S0-ALD-423

HOW TO TRADE

IN STOCKS:

The Livermore Formula For
Combining Time Element and Price

HOW TO TRADE IN STOCKS:

**The Livermore Formula For Combining
Time Element and Price**

by
Jesse L. Livermore

TRADERS PRESS ™
I N C O R P O R A T E D
P.O. BOX 6206
GREENVILLE, S.C. 29606

*Books and Gifts
for Investors and Traders*

Copyright©1940 by Jesse Livermore
Printed in the United States of America

ISBN: 0-934380-20-1

Originally published in 1940
Published May 1991

TRADERS PRESS™
P.O. BOX 6206
GREENVILLE, S.C. 29606

Books and Gifts
for Investors and Traders

HOW TO TRADE

IN STOCKS:

**The Livermore Formula For
Combining Time Element and Price**

TRADERS PRESS, INC.
P.O. BOX 6206
GREENVILLE, S.C. 29606

BOOKS FOR STOCK
AND COMMODITY
TRADERS

We have in stock most of the titles of interest to the technically oriented trader, as well as many other books of interest to traders in general. If we don't carry it in stock, we can generally quote you a price and have the book shipped to you direct from the publisher. Please write us at the above address, and we will gladly forward you our current "Trader's Catalog" by return mail.

EDWARD DOBSON
GREENVILLE, S.C.

HOW TO TRADE
IN STOCKS:
The Livermore Formula For
Combining Time Element and Price

INTRODUCTION

This classic book, first published in 1940, sets forth the specific trading techniques and methods used by the legendary Jesse Livermore. It has been out of print for many years and generally unavailable to the trading public. It completes the trilogy of books by and about Livermore (**Reminiscences of A Stock Operator; Jesse Livermore: Speculator King**; and **How To Trade In Stocks**). Anyone who has read the former two books about this famous and fascinating trader will doubtless want to complete his reading on Livermore with this volume. All three of these books are now published and maintained in print by **TRADERS PRESS.**

TRADERS PRESS specializes in the publication and sale of books of interest to the stock and commodity trader. To receive free sample commodity charts from our other publications and a copy of our current catalogue of over 200 books for traders, write us today at P.O. Box 6206, Greenville, S.C. 29606.

Greenville, S.C.
May 1991

Edward D. Dobson

TABLE OF CONTENTS

PREFACE

Even though more than a quarter-century has gone by since his death-by-suicide in 1940, Jesse Livermore frequently comes to "live" today in conversations occurring in the board-rooms and the back-offices located along that man-made — and fascinating — canyon known as "Wall Street."

This is quite understandable; for of all the colorful figures in stock market history Jesse Lauriston Livermore was the *only* operator who ever made and lost four stock market fortunes—each running into millions of dollars. What makes his roller-coaster financial past even more of a Wall Street wonder is the startling knowledge that everytime Livermore went bankrupt, his "hard-hearted" creditors (in the main, conservative—and dispassionate —stockbrokers) promptly let him off.

Tradition has it that the reason Livermore's creditors absolved him from his debts was simply that they couldn't afford to lose the commission business generated by his activities. But in any event such was his reputation that brokers and traders alike firmly believed Livermore to be the kind of genius who needed only a small bankroll, a stock ticker and a telephone to recoup his lost millions.

Jesse Livermore had more than just a reputation. He was a gifted man whose rare talents were busily employed for one unyielding purpose: the exciting business of speculation (profits from price changes).

To understand how Livermore came to be obsessed by the all-pervasive urge for wealth from price fluctuations, it is fitting to refer to his youth.

Born in South Acton, Massachusetts, in 1877, young Jesse (son of a poor plain-dirt farmer) speedily resented the aches and callouses of bucolic labors.

Hammered upon the forge of poverty, he began to dream of becoming rich—and famous. But most of all, he hungered to escape from the morass of the commonplace. He wanted to be a somebody.

To promote his ambitions, this farm boy (at fifteen) ran off to Boston, where he wound up as a board boy in Paine Webber's office. There, for a few dollars a week, he diligently chalked the ever-changing prices of stocks, bonds, and commodities onto a blackboard.

At first, these prices and their changes were quite meaningless to Jesse Livermore. But when he came to realize that every time a price changed somebody made money, he became solidly hooked on the concept of mastering the forecasting of such changes. It was not too long before he put his theories to the test. At lunch hour he began to haunt the local bucket shops (emporiums where bets were made on the price action of stocks and commodities, without of course the actual purchase or sale of the involved items). And soon he found himself scalping small profits, while often being "wiped out" with small losses.

One day Jesse's supervisor warned him to stay away from those "dens of iniquity"; or else. Jesse chose the "or else"—and was promptly fired. Thus ended the first—and the last—job he ever had. For the next forty-eight years Livermore operated as a lone wolf, selfishly seeking his own aggrandizement.

Shortly after he was fired, Jesse did so well in the Boston bucket shows that he was banned from doing business in that city. Thereupon he went out of town, where he hurt the bucketshop operators so badly they dubbed him with the sobriquet, "Boy Wonder." A few years after the turn of the century, Jesse Livermore (then in his twenties) told himself he was ready for the "big-time." Quietly he moved into New York City to prepare for his first big killing. This came along in the spring of 1906, when Livermore, on a tip from Boston Lawson, went short of Union Pacific.

Tall, slim, blond-haired—and as dignified-looking as a college president—the icy-eyed Mr. Livermore hardly batted an eyelash as the price of Union Pacific inexorably began to rise—and he began to be seriously squeezed. Obviously, the well-intentioned tip he had received seemed to be turning sour, but Livermore, trapped, with remarkable naivete, stoically held his ground.

Luckily for Livermore, his first large-scale speculation worked out handsomely *only* because of a miracle. In April of 1906, the world was shocked by the San Francisco earthquake. The market broke badly. And two days thereafter, Livermore covered his shorts for a profit of more than a quarter-million.

The financially happy outcome of what at first appeared to be a tragedy from a tip taught Livermore his first important lesson: "Never act on tips." The experience also taught him to seek a more sensible approach to the business of assuming market risk. He began to experiment along the lines of working out a thinking-man's stock market system.

During the decades that followed, Jesse Livermore sharpened his market tools, concentrating on an accurate method of price-analysis as a basis for price-prediction. Painfully, he learned from his own mistakes—and from the mistakes of other large-scale operators. For many years he stubbornly fought off publishers and tout-sheet operators alike, who pleaded with him to publish the secrets of his stock market methods. Meanwhile, Livermore patiently perfected his "key"—with the thought in mind that when it had proved to be successful at least 60% of the time he would then air it to the investment world.

What motivated him, in 1939, to finally share his

secrets with his fellow men was more than the money he hoped to realize from the sale of his book. For all during the years that Livermore worked on his *Key* system he yearned desperately to make his life meaningful; not only to himself, but also to his fellow Americans—people who he knew played the stock market against professionals holding marked cards. And so Jesse Livermore wrote the revealing book that follows.

Man's most powerful weapon for self-betterment is the intelligent application of the lessons of personal experience, Jesse Livermore knew this just as he also knew that learning and knowledge are not sold in the same store. For almost fifty continuous years, day-in and day-out, he absorbed lessons from stock market activity. Trenchantly he processed them inside a mind that any sharp Yankee trader would have been proud to own. And he set down his findings in a readable fashion—so that all could understand what he was trying to say.

Whether or not risk-takers reading this work will make money by applying the lessons of Jesse Livermore to today's markets is of course a debatable question. But *every reader* of this book will be enriched by its wisdom, its sensible "rules"—and the signposts in it pointing up the dangers to risk-capital as represented by changing prices. Chances are this book's readers will turn to it time and again, as if to an old friend, for its richly informative pages can often be comforting—and consoling. Assuredly, it will help make anyone's stock market approach more pleasurable.

PAUL SARNOFF

I

THE CHALLENGE OF SPECULATION

THE game of speculation is the most uniformly fascinating game in the world. But it is not a game for the stupid, the mentally lazy, the man of inferior emotional balance, nor for the get-rich-quick adventurer. They will die poor.

Over a long period of years I have rarely attended a dinner party including strangers that someone did not sit down beside me and after the usual pleasantries inquire:

"How can I make some money in the market?"

In my younger days I would go to considerable pains to explain all the difficulties faced by the one who simply wishes to take quick and easy money out of the market; or through courteous evasiveness I would work my way out of the snare. In later years my answer has been a blunt "I don't know."

It is difficult to exercise patience with such people. In the first place, the inquiry is not a compliment to the man who has made a scientific study of investment and speculation. It would be as fair for the layman to ask an attorney or a surgeon:

"How can I make some quick money in law or surgery?"

I have come to the conviction, however, that larger numbers of people interested in stock-market investment and speculation would be willing to work and study to attain sensible results, if they had a guide or signpost pointing the right direction. And it is for them that this book is written.

It is my purpose to include some of the highlights of a lifetime of speculative experience—a record of some of the failures and successes and the lessons that each has taught. Out of it all emerges my theory of time element in trading, which I regard as the most important factor in successful speculation.

But before we go further, let me warn you that the fruits of your success will be in direct ratio to the honesty and sincerity of your own effort in keeping your own records, doing your own thinking, and reaching your own conclusions. You cannot wisely read a book on "How to Keep Fit" and leave the physical exercises to another. Nor can you delegate to another the task of keeping your records, if you are to follow faithfully my formula for combining the time element and prices, as set forth in subsequent pages.

I can only light the way, and I shall be happy, if through my guidance, you are able to take more money out of the stock market than you put in.

In this book, I present to that portion of the public, which at times may be speculatively inclined, some points and ideas which have been garnered during my many years as an investor and speculator. Anyone who is inclined to speculate should look at speculation as a business and treat it as such and not regard it as a pure gamble as so many people are apt to do. If I am correct in the premise that speculation is a business in itself, those engaging in that business should determine to learn and understand it to the best of their ability with informative data available. In the forty years which I have devoted to making speculation a successful business venture, I have discovered and still am discovering new rules to apply to that business.

On many occasions I have gone to bed wondering why I had not been able to foresee a certain imminent move, and awakened in the early hours of the ensuing morning with a new idea formulated. I was impatient for the morning to arrive in order to start checking over my records of past movements to determine whether the new idea had merit. In most cases it was far from being 100% right, but what good there was in it was stored away in my subconscious mind. Perhaps, later, another idea would take form and I would immediately set to work checking it over.

In time these various ideas began to crystallize and I was able to develop a concrete method of keeping records in such a form that I could use them as a guide.

My theory and practical application have proved to my satisfaction that nothing new ever occurs in the business of speculating or investing in securities or commodities. There are times when one should speculate, and just as surely there are times when one should not speculate. There is a very true adage: "You can beat a horse race, but you can't beat the races." So it is with market operations. There are times when money can be made investing and speculating in stocks, but money cannot consistently be made trading every day or every week during the year. Only the foolhardy will try it. It just is not in the cards and cannot be done.

To invest or speculate successfully, one must form an opinion as to what the next move of importance will be in a given stock. Speculation is nothing more than anticipating coming movements. In order to anticipate correctly, one must have a definite basis for that anticipation. For instance, analyze in your own mind the effect, marketwise, that a certain piece of news which has been made public may have in relation to the market. Try to anticipate the psychological effect of this particular item on the mind of the public— particularly that portion of the public which primarily is interested. If you believe it likely to have a definite bullish or bearish effect marketwise, don't trust your own opinion and back your judgment *until the action of the market itself confirms* your *opinion* because the effect marketwise may not be as pronounced as you are inclined to believe it should be. To illustrate: After the market has been in a definite trend for a given period, a bullish or bearish piece of news may not have the slightest effect on the market. The market itself at the time may be in an overbought or oversold condition, in which case the effect of that particular news would certainly be ignored. At such times the recording value of past performances under similar conditions becomes of inestimable value to the investor or speculator. At such times he must entirely ignore personal opinion and apply strict attention to the *action of the market itself. Markets are never wrong* —opinions often are. The latter are of no value to the investor or speculator unless the market acts in accordance with his ideas. No one man, or group of men, can make or break a market today. One may form an opinion regarding a certain stock and believe that it is going to have a pronounced move, either up or down, and eventually be correct in his opinion but will lose money by presuming or acting on his opinion too soon. Believing it to be right, he acts immediately, only to find that after he has made his commitment, the stock goes the other way. The market becomes narrow, he becomes tired and goes out. Perhaps a few days later it begins to look all right, and in he goes again, but no sooner has he re-entered it than it turns against him once more. Once more he begins to doubt his opinion and sells out. Finally the move starts up. Having been too hasty and having made two erroneous commitments, he loses courage. It is also likely that he has made other commitments and is not in a position to assume more. Thus, by the time the real move in the stock he jumped into prematurely is on, he is out of it.

The point I would here emphasize is that after forming a definite opinion with respect to a certain stock or stocks—do not be too anxious to get into it. Wait and watch the action of that stock or stocks marketwise. Have a fundamental basis to be guided by. Say, for instance, a stock is selling around $25.00 and has been holding within a range of $22.00 to $28.00 for a considerable period. Assuming that you believe that the stock should eventually sell at $50.00, and it is $25.00 at the time, and in your opinion it will sell at $50.00, have patience and wait until the stock becomes active, until it makes a new high, say around $30.00. You will then know that marketwise you have been justified. The stock must have gone into a very strong position, or it would not have reached $30.00. Having done so, it is altogether likely that it is on its way to a very definite advance—the move is on. That is the time for you to back your opinion. Don't let the fact that you did not buy at $25.00 cause you any aggravation. The chances are if you had, you would have become tired of waiting and would have been out of it when the move started, because having once gotten out at a lower price, you would have become disgruntled and would not have gone back in when you should have.

Experience has proved to me that the real money made in speculating has been in commitments in a stock or commodity showing a profit right from the start. Later on, when some examples of my

trading operations are given, you will notice I made
my first trade at the psychological time—that is,
at a time where the force of the movement was so
strong that it simply had to carry through. Not on
my operation but because the force was so strong
behind that particular stock. It simply had to and
did go. There have been many times when I, like
many other speculators, have not had the patience
to await the sure thing. I wanted to have an interest at all times. You may say: "With all your experience, why did you allow yourself to do so?"
The answer to that is that I am human and subject
to human weakness. Like all speculators, I permitted impatience to out-maneuver good judgment. Speculation is very similar to playing a game
of cards, whether it be poker, bridge or any similar
game. Each of us is possessed with the common
weakness of wanting to have an interest in every
jackpot, and we certainly would like to play every
hand at bridge. It is this human frailty which we
all possess in some degree that becomes the investor's and speculator's greatest enemy and will eventually, if not safeguarded, bring about his downfall.
It is a human trait to be hopeful and equally so to
be fearful, but when you inject hope and fear into
the business of speculation, you are faced with a
very formidable hazard, because you are apt to get
the two confused and in reverse positions.

As an illustration: You buy a stock at $30.00.
The next day it has a quick run-up to $32.00 or
$32.50. You immediately become fearful that if
you don't take the profit, the next day you may see
it fade away—so out you go with a small profit,
when that is the very time you should entertain all
the hope in the world. Why should you worry
about losing two points' profit which you did not
have the previous day? If you can make two points'
profit in one day, you might make two or three the

next, and perhaps five more the next week. As long as a stock is acting right, and the market is right, do not be in a hurry to take a profit. You know you are right, because if you were not, you would have no profit at all. Let it ride and ride along with it. It may grow into a very large profit, and as long as the *action of the market* does not give you any cause to worry, have the courage of your convictions and stay with it. On the other hand, suppose you buy a stock at $30.00, and the next day it goes to $28.00, showing a two-point loss. You would not be fearful that the next day would possibly see a three-point loss or more. No, you would regard it merely as a temporary reaction, feeling certain that the next day it would recover its loss. But that is the time that you should be worried. That two-point loss could be followed by two points the next day, or possibly five or ten within the next week or two. That is when you should be fearful, because if you do not get out, you might be forced to take a much greater loss later on. That is the time you should protect yourself by selling your stock before the loss assumes larger proportions.

Profits always take care of themselves but losses never do. The speculator has to insure himself against considerable losses by taking the first small loss. In so doing, he keeps his account in order so that at some future time, when he has a constructive idea, he will be in a position to go into another deal, taking on the same amount of stock as he had when he was wrong. The speculator has to be his own insurance broker, and the only way he can continue in business is to guard his capital account and never permit himself to lose enough to jeopardize his operations at some future date when his market judgment is correct. While I believe that the successful investor or speculator must have well-advanced reasons for making commitments on either side of the market, I feel he must also be able through some form of a specific guide to determine when to make his first commitments.

Let me repeat, there are definitely certain times when a movement really gets under way, and I firmly believe that anyone who has the instinct of a speculator and has the patience, can devise a specific method to be used as a guide which will permit him to judge correctly when to make his initial commitment. Successful speculation is anything but a mere guess. To be consistently successful, an investor or speculator must have rules to guide him. Certain guides which I utilize may be of no value to anyone else. Why is that so? If they are of inestimable value to me, why should they not serve you equally well? The answer to that is— no guide can be 100% right. If I use a certain guide, my own pet one, I know what should be the result. If my stock does not act as I anticipated, I immediately determine the time is not yet ripe— so I close out my commitment. Perhaps a few days later my guide indicates I should get in again, so back I go, and probably this time it is 100% correct. I believe anyone who will take the time and trouble to study price movements should in time be able to develop a guide, which will aid him in future operations or investments. In this book I present some points which I have found valuable in my own speculative operations.

A great many traders keep charts or records of averages. They chase them around, up and down, and there is no question that these charts of averages do point out a definite trend at times. Personally, charts have never appealed to me. I think they are altogether too confusing. Nevertheless, I am just as much of a fanatic in keeping records as other people are in maintaining charts. They may be right, and I may be wrong.

My preference for records is due to the fact that my recording method gives me a clear picture of what is happening. But it was not until I began to take into consideration the time element that my records really became useful in helping me to anticipate coming movements of importance. I believe that by keeping proper records and taking the time element into consideration—and I shall explain this in detail later—*one can with a fair degree of accuracy forecast coming movements of importance*. But it takes patience to do so.

Familiarize yourself with a stock, or different groups of stocks, and if you figure the time element correctly in conjunction with your records, sooner or later you will be able to determine when a major move is due. If you read your records correctly, you will pick the leading stock in any group. You must, I repeat, keep your own records. You must put down your own figures. Don't let anyone else do it for you. You will be surprised how many new ideas you will formulate in so doing, ideas which no one else could give to you, because they are your discovery, your secret, and you should keep them your secret.

I offer in this book some DON'TS for investors and speculators. One of the primary rules is that one should never permit speculative ventures to run into investments. Investors often take tremendous losses for no other reason than that their stocks are bought and paid for.

How often have you heard an investor say: "I don't have to worry about fluctuations or margin calls. I never speculate. When I buy stocks, I buy them for an investment, and if they go down, eventually they will come back."

But unhappily for such investors many stocks bought at a time when they were deemed good investments have later met with drastically changed conditions. Hence such so-called "investment stocks" frequently become purely speculative. Some go out of existence altogether. The original "investment" evaporates into thin air along with the capital of the investor. This occurrence is due to the failure to realize that so-called "investments" may be called upon in the future to face a new set of conditions which would jeopardize the earning capacity of the stock, originally bought for a permanent investment. Before the investor learns of this changed situation, the value of his investment is already greatly depreciated. Therefore the investor must guard his capital account just as the successful speculator does in his speculative ventures. If this were done, those who like to call themselves "investors" would not be forced to become unwilling speculators of the future—nor would trust fund accounts depreciate so much in their value.

You will recall not so many years ago it was considered safer to have your money invested in the New York, New Haven & Hartford Railroad than to have it in a bank. On April 28, 1902, New Haven was selling at $255 a share. In December of 1906, Chicago, Milwaukee & St. Paul sold at $199.62. In January of that same year Chicago Northwestern sold at $240 a share. On February 9 of that year Great Northern Railway sold at $348 a share. All were paying good dividends.

Look at those "investments" today: On January 2, 1940, they were quoted at the following prices: New York, New Haven & Hartford Railroad $0.50 per share; Chicago Northwestern at $5/16$, which is about $0.31 per share; Great Northern Railway at $26.62½ per share. On January 2, 1940, there was no quotation for Chicago, Milwaukee & St. Paul—but on January 5, 1940, it was quoted at $0.25 per share.

It would be simple to run down the list of hundreds of stocks which, in my time, have been considered gilt-edge investments, and which today are worth little or nothing. Thus, great investments tumble, and with them the fortunes of so-called conservative investors in the continuous distribution of wealth.

Speculators in stock markets have lost money. But I believe it is a safe statement that the money lost by speculation alone is small compared with the gigantic sums lost by so-called investors who have let their investments ride.

From my viewpoint, the investors are the big gamblers. They make a bet, stay with it, and if it goes wrong, they lose it all. The speculator might buy at the same time. But if he is an intelligent speculator, he will recognize—if he keeps records—the danger signal warning him all is not well. He will, by acting promptly, hold his losses to a minimum and await a more favorable opportunity to re-enter the market.

When a stock starts sliding downward, no one can tell how far it will go. Nor can anyone guess the ultimate top on a stock in a broad upward movement. A few thoughts should be kept uppermost in mind. One is: Never sell a stock, because it seems high-priced. You may watch the stock go from 10 to 50 and decide that it is selling at too high a level. That is the time to determine what is to prevent it from starting at 50 and going to 150 under favorable earning conditions and good corporate management. Many have lost their capital funds by selling a stock short after a long upward movement, when it "seemed too high."

Conversely, never buy a stock because it has had a big decline from its previous high. The likelihood is that the decline is based on a very good reason. That stock may still be selling at an extremely high price—even if the current level seems low. Try to forget its past high range and study it on the basis of the formula which combines timing and price.

It may surprise many to know that in my method of trading, when I see by my records that an upward trend is in progress, I become a buyer as soon as a stock makes a new high on its movement, after having had a normal reaction. The same applies whenever I take the short side. Why? Because I am following the trend at the time. My records signal me to go ahead!

I never buy on reactions or go short on rallies.

One other point: It is foolhardy to make a second trade, if your first trade shows you a loss. Never average losses. Let that thought be written indelibly upon your mind.

II

WHEN DOES A STOCK ACT RIGHT?

STOCKS, like individuals, have character and personality. Some are high-strung, nervous, and jumpy; others are forthright, direct, logical. One comes to know and respect individual securities. Their action is predictable under varying sets of conditions.

Markets never stand still. They are very dull at times, but they are not resting at one price. They are either moving up or down a fraction. When a stock gets into a definite trend, it works automatically and consistently along certain lines throughout the progress of its move.

At the beginning of the move you will notice a very large volume of sales with gradually advancing prices for a few days. Then what I term a "Normal Reaction" will occur. On that reaction the sales volume will be much less than on the previous days of its advance. Now that little reaction is only normal. Never be afraid of the normal movement. But be very fearful of abnormal movements.

In a day or two activity will start again, and the volume will increase. If it is a real movement, in a short space of time the natural, normal reaction will have been recovered, and the stock will be selling in new high territory. That movement should continue strong for a few days with only minor daily reactions. Sooner or later it will reach a point where it is due for another normal reaction. When it occurs, it should be on the same lines as the first reaction, because that is the natural way any stock will act when it is in a definite trend. At the first part of a movement of this kind the distance above the previous high point to the next high point is not very great. But as time goes on you will notice that it is making much faster headway on the upside.

Let me illustrate: Take a stock that starts at 50. On the first leg of the movement it might gradually sell up to 54. A day or two of normal reaction might carry it back to 52½ or so. Three days later it is on its way again. In that time it might go up to 59 or 60 before the normal reaction would occur. But instead of reacting, say, only a point or a point and one-half, a natural reaction from that level could easily be 3 points. When it resumes its advance again in a few days, you will notice that the volume of sales at that time is not nearly as large as it was at the beginning of the move. The stock is becoming harder to buy. That being the case, the next points in the movement will be much more rapid than before. The stock could easily go from the previous high of 60 to 68 or 70 without encountering a natural reaction. When that normal reaction does occur, it could be more severe. It could easily react down to 65 and still have only a normal decline. But assuming that the reaction was five points or thereabouts, it should not be many days before the advance would be resumed, and the stock should be selling at a brand new high price. And that is where the time element comes in.

Don't let the stock go stale on you. After attaining a goodly profit, you must have patience, but don't let patience create a frame of mind that ignores the danger signals.

The stock starts up again, and it has a rise of six or seven points in one day, followed the next day by perhaps eight to ten points—with great activity—but during the last hour of the day all of a sudden it has an abnormal break of seven or eight points. The next morning it extends its reaction another point or so, and then once more starts to advance, closing very strong. But the following day, for some reason, it does not carry through.

This is an immediate danger signal. All during the progress of the move it had nothing but natural and normal reactions. Then all of a sudden an abnormal reaction occurs—and by "abnormal" I mean a reaction *in one day* of six or more points from an extreme price made in that same day—something it has not had before, and when something happens abnormally stock-marketwise, it is flashing you a danger signal which must not be ignored.

You have had patience to stay with the stock all during its natural progress. Now have the courage and good sense to honor the danger signal and step aside.

I do not say that these danger signals are always correct because, as stated before, no rules applying to stock fluctuations are 100% right. But if you pay attention to them consistently, in the long run you will profit immensely.

A speculator of great genius once told me: "When I see a danger signal handed to me, I don't argue with it. I get out! A few days later, if everything looks all right, I can always go back in again. Thereby I have saved myself a lot of worry and money. I figure it out this way. If I were walking along a railroad track and saw an express train coming at me sixty miles an hour, I would not be damned fool enough not to get off the track and let the train go by. After it had passed, I could always get back on the track again, if I desired."

I have always remembered that as a graphic bit of speculative wisdom.

Every judicious speculator is on the alert for danger signals. Curiously, the trouble with most speculators is that something inside of them keeps them from mustering enough courage to close out their commitment when they should. They hesitate and during that period of hesitation they watch the market go many points against them. Then they say: "On the next rally I'll get out!" When the next rally comes, as it will eventually, they forget what they intended to do, because in their opinion the market is acting fine again. However, that rally was only a temporary swing which soon plays out, and then the market starts to go down in earnest. And they are in it—due to their hesitation. If they had been using a guide, it would have told them what to do, not only saving them a lot of money but eliminating their worries.

Again let me say, the human side of every person is the greatest enemy of the average investor or speculator. Why shouldn't a stock rally after it starts down from a big advance? Of course it will rally from some level. But why hope it is going to rally at just the time you want it to rally? Chances are it won't, and if it does, the vacillating type of speculator may not take advantage of it.

What I am trying to make clear to that part of the public which desires to regard speculation as a serious business, and I wish deliberately to reiterate it, is that wishful thinking must be banished; that one cannot be successful by speculating every day or every week; that there are only a few times a year, possibly four or five, when you should allow yourself to make any commitment at all. In the interims you are letting the market shape itself for the next big movement.

If you have timed the movement correctly, your

first commitment will show you a profit at the start. From then on, all that is required of you is to be alert, watching for the appearance of the danger signal to tell you to step aside and convert paper profits into real money.

Remember this: When you are doing nothing, those speculators who feel they must trade day in and day out, are laying the foundation for your next venture. You will reap benefits from their mistakes.

Speculation is far too exciting. Most people who speculate hound the brokerage offices or receive frequent telephone calls, and after the business day they talk markets with friends at all gatherings. The ticker or translux is always on their minds. They are so engrossed with the minor ups and downs that they miss the big movements. Almost invariably the vast majority have commitments on the wrong side when the broad trend swings under way. The speculator who insists on trying to profit from daily minor movements will never be in a position to take advantage of the next important change marketwise when it occurs.

Such weaknesses can be corrected by keeping and studying records of stock price movements and how they occur, and by taking the time element carefully into account.

Many years ago I heard of a remarkably successful speculator who lived in the California mountains and received quotations three days old. Two or three times a year he would call on his San Francisco broker and begin writing out orders to buy or sell, depending upon his market position. A friend of mine, who spent time in the broker's office, became curious and made inquiries. His astonishment mounted when he learned of the man's extreme detachment from market facilities, his rare visits, and, on occasions, his tremendous volume of trade. Finally he was introduced, and in the course of conversation inquired of this man from the mountains how he could keep track of the stock market at such an isolated distance.

"Well," he replied, "I make speculation a business. I would be a failure if I were in the confusion of things and let myself be distracted by minor changes. I like to be away where I can think. You see, I keep a record of what has happened, after it has happened, and it gives me a rather clear picture of what markets are doing. Real movements do not end the day they start. It takes time to complete the end of a genuine movement. By being up in the mountains I am in a position to give these movements all the time they need. But a day comes when I get some prices out of the paper and put them down in my records. I notice the prices I record are not conforming to the same pattern of movements that has been apparent for some time. Right then I make up my mind. I go to town and get busy."

That happened many years ago. Consistently, the man from the mountains, over a long period of time, drew funds abundantly from the stock market. He was something of an inspiration to me. I went to work harder than ever trying to blend the time element with all the other data I had compiled. By constant effort I was able to bring my records into a co-ordination that aided me to a surprising degree in anticipating coming movements.

FOLLOW THE LEADERS

THERE is always the temptation in the stock market, after a period of success, to become careless or excessively ambitious. Then it requires sound common sense and clear thinking to keep what you have. But it is not necessary to lose your money, once you have acquired it, if you will hold fast to sound principles.

We know that prices move up and down. They always have and they always will. My theory is that behind these major movements is an irresistible force. That is all one needs to know. It is not well to be too curious about all the reasons behind price movements. You risk the danger of clouding your mind with non-essentials. Just recognize that the movement is there and take advantage of it by steering your speculative ship along with the tide. Do not argue with the condition, and most of all, do not try to combat it.

Remember too that it is dangerous to start spreading out all over the market. By this I mean, do not have an interest in too many stocks at one time. It is much easier to watch a few than many. I made that mistake years ago and it cost me money.

Another mistake I made was to permit myself to turn completely bearish or bullish on the whole market, because one stock in some particular group had plainly reversed its course from the general market trend. Before making a new commitment, I should have been patient and awaited the time, when some stock in another group had indicated to me that its decline or advance had ended. In time, other stocks would clearly give the same indication. Those are the cues I should have waited for.

But instead of doing so, I felt the costly urge of getting busy in the whole market. Thus I permitted the hankering for activity to replace common sense and judgment. Of course I made money on my trades in the first and second groups. But I chipped away a substantial part of it by entering other groups before the zero hour had arrized.

Back in the wild bull markets of the late twenties I saw clearly that the advance in the copper stocks had come to an end. A short time later the advance in the motor group reached its zenith. Because the bull market in those two groups had terminated, I soon arrived at the faulty conclusion that I could safely sell everything. I should hate to tell you the amount of money I lost by acting upon that premise.

While I was piling up huge paper profits on my copper and motor deals, I lost even more in the next six months trying to find the top of the utility group. Eventually this and other groups reached their peaks. By that time Anaconda was selling 50 points below its previous high and the motor stocks in about the same ratio.

What I wish to impress upon you is the fact that when you clearly see a move coming in a particular group, act upon it. But do not let yourself act in the same way in some other group, until you plainly see signs that the second group is in a position to follow suit. Have patience and wait. In time you will get the same tip-off in other groups that you received in the first group. Just don't spread out over the market.

Confine your studies of movements to the prominent stocks of the day. If you cannot make money out of the leading active issues, you are not going to make money out of the stock market as a whole.

Just as styles in women's gowns and hats and costume jewelry are forever changing with time, the old leaders of the stock market are dropped and new ones rise up to take their places. Years ago the chief leaders were the railroads, American Sugar, and Tobacco. Then came the steels, and American Sugar and Tobacco were nudged into the background. Then came the motors, and so on up to the present time. Today we have only four groups in the position of dominating the market: steels, motors, aircraft stocks, and mail orders. As they go, so goes the whole market. In the course of time new leaders will come to the front; some of the old leaders will be dropped. It will always be that way as long as there is a stock market.

Definitely it is not safe to try to keep account of too many stocks at one time. You will become entangled and confused. Try to analyze comparatively few groups. You will find it is much easier to obtain a true picture that way than if you tried to dissect the whole market. If you analyze correctly the course of two stocks in the four prominent groups, you need not worry about what the rest are going to do. It becomes the old story of "follow the leader." Keep mentally flexible. Remember the leaders of today may not be the leaders two years from now.

Today, in my records I keep four individual groups. That does not mean I am trading in all of the groups at the same time. But I have a genuine purpose in mind.

When I first became interested in the movement of prices long, long ago, I decided to test my ability to anticipate correctly forthcoming movements. I recorded fictitious trades in a little book which was always with me. In the course of time, I made my first actual trade. I never will forget that trade. I had half-interest in a purchase of five shares of Chicago, Burlington & Quincy Railway Stock, bought with a friend of mine, and my share of the profit amounted to $3.12. From that time on I became a speculator on my own.

Under conditions as they currently exist, I do not believe that a speculator of the old type who traded in huge volume has much chance of success. When I say a speculator of the old type, I am thinking of the days when markets were very broad and liquid and when a speculator might take a position with 5,000 or 10,000 shares of a stock and move in and out without greatly influencing the price.

After taking his initial position, if the stock acted right, the speculator could safely add to his line from that time forward. In former times, if his judgment proved faulty, he could move out of his position easily without taking too serious a loss. But today, if his first position proved untenable, he would suffer a devastating loss in changing about because of the comparative narrowness of the market.

On the other hand, as I have implied previously, the speculator of today who has the patience and judgment to wait the proper time for acting has, in my opinion, a better chance of cashing in good profits eventually, because the current market does not lend itself to so many artificial movements, movements that far too frequently in the old days jarred all scientific calculations out of kilter.

It is obvious, therefore, that in light of conditions

which exist today, no speculator who is intelligent will permit himself to operate on that scale which was more or less a commonplace some years ago. He will study a limited number of groups and of leaders in those groups. He will learn to look before he leaps. For a new age of markets has been ushered in—an age that offers safer opportunities for the reasonable, studious, competent investor and speculator.

IV

MONEY IN THE HAND

WHEN you are handling surplus income do not delegate the task to anyone.

Whether you are dealing in millions or in thousands the same principal lesson applies. It is your money. It will remain with you just so long as you guard it. Faulty speculation is one of the most certain ways of losing it.

Blunders by incompetent speculators cover a wide scale. I have warned against averaging losses. That is a most common practice. Great numbers of people will buy a stock, let us say at 50, and two or three days later if they can buy it at 47 they are seized with the urge to average down by buying another hundred shares, making a price of 48½ on all. Having bought at 50 and being concerned over a three-point loss on a hundred shares, what rhyme or reason is there in adding another hundred shares and having the double worry when the price hits 44? At that point there would be a $600 loss on the first hundred shares and a $300 loss on the second hundred shares.

If one is to apply such an unsound principle, he should keep on averaging by buying two hundred shares at 44, then four hundred at 41, eight hundred at 38, sixteen hundred at 35, thirty-two hundred at 32, sixty-four hundred at 29 and so on. How many speculators could stand such pressure? Yet if the policy is sound it should not be abandoned. Of course abnormal moves such as the one indicated do not happen often. But it is just such abnormal moves against which the speculator must guard to avoid disaster.

So, at the risk of repetition and preaching, let me urge you to avoid averaging down.

I know but one sure tip from a broker. It is your margin call. When it reaches you, close your account. You are on the wrong side of the market. Why send good money after bad? Keep that good money for another day. Risk it on something more attractive than an obviously losing deal.

A successful businessman extends credit to various customers but would dislike to sell his entire output to one customer. The larger the number of customers the more widely the risk is spread. Just so, a person engaged in the business of speculation should risk only a limited amount of capital on any one venture. Cash to the speculator is as merchandise on the shelves of the merchant.

One major mistake of all speculators is the urge to enrich themselves in too short a time. Instead of taking two or three years to make 500% on their capital, they try to do it in two or three months. Now and then they succeed. But do such daring traders keep it? They do not. Why? Because it is unhealthy money, rolling in rapidly, and stopping for but a short visit. The speculator in such instances loses his sense of balance. He says: "If I can make 500% on my capital in two months, think what I will do in the next two! I will make a fortune."

Such speculators are never satisfied. They continue to shoot the works until somewhere a cog slips, something happens—something drastic, unforeseen, and devastating. At length comes that final margin call from the broker, the call that cannot be met, and this type of plunger goes out like a lamp. He may plead with the broker for a little more time, or if he is not too unfortunate, he may have saved a nest-egg permitting a modest new start.

Businessmen opening a shop or a store would not expect to make over 25% on their investment the first year. But to people who enter the speculative field 25% is nothing. They are looking for 100%. And their calculations are faulty; they fail to make speculation a business and run it on business principles.

Here is another little point that might well be remembered. A speculator should make it a rule each time he closes out a successful deal to take one-half of his profits and lock this sum up in a safe deposit box. The only money that is ever taken out of Wall Street by speculators is the money they draw out of their accounts after closing a successful deal.

I recall one day in Palm Beach. I left New York with a fairly large short position open. A few days after my arrival in Palm Beach the market had a severe break. That was an opportunity to cash "paper profits" into real money—and I did.

After the market closed I gave a message to the telegraph operator to tell the New York office to send immediately to my bank one million dollars to be deposited to my credit. The telegraph operator almost passed out. After sending the message, he asked if he might keep that slip. I inquired why. He said he had been an operator for twenty years and that was the first message he ever sent asking a broker to deposit in a bank money for the account of a customer. He went on:

"Thousands and thousands of messages have gone over the wire from brokers demanding margins from customers. But never before one like yours. I want to show it to the boys."

The only time the average speculator can draw

money from his brokerage account is when he has no position open or when he has an excessive equity. He won't draw it out when the markets are going against him because he needs all his capital for margin. He won't draw it out after closing a successful deal because he says to himself:

"Next time I'll make twice as much."

Consequently most speculators rarely see the money. To them the money is nothing real, nothing tangible. For years, after a successful deal was closed, I made it a habit to draw out cash. I used to draw it out at the rate of $200,000 or $300,000 a clip. It is a good policy. It has a psychological value. Make it a policy to do that. Count the money over. I did. I knew I had something in my hand. I felt it. It was real.

Money in a broker's account or in a bank account is not the same as if you feel it in your own fingers once in a while. Then it means something. There is a sense of possession that makes you just a little bit less inclined to take headstrong chances of losing your gains. So have a look at your real money once in a while, particularly between your market deals.

There is too much looseness in these matters on the part of the average speculator.

When a speculator is fortunate enough to double his original capital he should at once draw out one-half of his profit to be set aside for reserve. This policy has been tremendously helpful to me on many occasions. I only regret that I have not observed it throughout my career. In some places it would have smoothed the path.

I never have been able to make a dollar outside of Wall Street. But I have lost many millions of dollars, which I had taken from Wall Street, "investing" in other ventures. I have in mind real estate in the Florida boom, oil wells, airplane manufacturing, and the perfecting and marketing of products based on new inventions. Always I lost every cent.

In one of these outside ventures which had whipped up my enthusiasm I sought to interest a friend of mine to the extent of $50,000. He listened to my story very attentively. When I had finished he said: "Livermore, you will never make a success in any business outside of your own. Now if you want $50,000 with which to speculate it is yours for the asking. But please speculate and stay away from business."

Next morning, to my surprise, the mail brought a check for that amount which I did not need.

The lesson here again is that speculation itself is a business and should be so viewed by all. Do not permit yourself to be influenced by excitement, flattery or temptation. Keep in mind that brokers sometimes innocently become the undoing of many speculators. Brokers are in the business to make commissions. They cannot make commissions unless customers trade. The more trade, the more commissions. The speculator wants to trade and the broker not only is willing but too often encourages over-trading. The uninformed speculator regards the broker as his friend and is soon over-trading.

Now if the speculator were smart enough to know at just which time he should over-trade, the practice would be justified. He may know at times when he could or should over-trade. But once acquiring the habit, very few speculators are smart enough to stop. They are carried away, and they lose that peculiar sense of balance so essential to success. They never think of the day when they will be wrong. But that day arrives. The easy money takes wing, and another speculator is broke.

Never make any trade unless you know you can do so with financial safety.

V

THE PIVOTAL POINT

WHENEVER I have had the patience to wait for the market to arrive at what I call a "Pivotal Point" before I started to trade, I have always made money in my operations.

Why?

Because I then commenced my play just at the psychological time at the beginning of a move. I never had a loss to worry about for the simple reason that I acted promptly and started to accumulate my line right at the time my guide told me to do so. All I had to do thereafter was just sit tight and let the market run its course, knowing if I did so, the action of the market itself would give me in due time the signal to take my profits. And whenever I had the nerve and the patience to wait for the signal, it invariably did just that. It has always been my experience that I never benefited much from a move if I did not get in at somewhere near the beginning of that move. And the reason is that I missed the backlog of profit which is very necessary to provide the courage and patience to sit through a move until the end comes—and to stay through any minor reactions or rallies which were bound to occur from time to time before the movement had completed its course.

Just as markets in time will give you a positive

tip when to get in—if you have patience to wait—
they will just as surely give you a tip-off when to
get out. *"Rome was not built in a day," and no real
movement of importance ends in one day or in one
week.* It takes time for it to run its logical course.
It is significant that a large part of a market movement occurs in the last forty-eight hours of a play,
and that is the most important time to be in it.

For example: Take a stock which has been in a
Downward Trend for quite some time and reaches
a low point of 40. Then it has a quick rally in a
few days to 45, then it backs and fills for a week in
a range of a few points, and then it starts to extend
its rally until it reaches 49½. The market becomes
dull and inactive for a few days. Then one day it
becomes active again and goes down 3 or 4 points,
and keeps on going down until it reaches a price
near its Pivotal Point of 40. Right here is the time
the market should be watched carefully, because if
the stock is really going to resume its Downward
Trend in earnest it should sell below its Pivotal
Point of 40 by three points or more before it has
another rally of importance. If it fails to pierce 40
it is an indication to buy as soon as it rallies 3
points from the low price made on that reaction.
If the 40 point has been pierced but not by the
proper extent of 3 points, then it should be bought
as soon as it advances to 43.

If either one of these two things happen, you
will find, in the majority of cases, that it marks the
beginning of a new trend, and if the trend is going
to be confirmed in a positive manner, it will continue to advance and reach a price over the Pivotal
point of 49½—by 3 points or more.

I do not use the words "bullish" or "bearish" in
defining trends of the market, because I think so
many people, when they hear the words "bullish"
or "bearish" spoken of marketwise immediately

think that is the course the market is going to take for a very long time.

Well-defined trends of that kind do not occur very often—only once in about four or five years—but during that time there are many well-defined trends which last for a comparatively short time. I consequently use the words "Upward Trend" and "Downward Trend," because they fully express what is going on at that specific time. Moreover, if you make a purchase because you think the market is going into an Upward Trend, and then a few weeks later come to the conclusion the market is heading into a Downward Trend, you will find it much easier to accept the reversal in trend than if you had a confirmed opinion that the market was definitely in a "bullish" or "bearish" stage.

The Livermore Method of recording prices in conjunction with the time element is the result of over thirty years of study of principles which would serve me in forming a basic guide for the next important movement.

After making my first record, I found it did not help me to any great extent. Weeks later I had a new thought which aroused me to fresh endeavors, only to find out that, while it was an improvement over the first one, it still did not give me the desired information. Successively new thoughts would come to mind, and I would make a set of new records. Gradually, after making many of these, I began to develop ideas I did not have before, and each succeeding record I made began to shape itself into better form. But from the time I started to merge the time element with price movements, my records began to talk to me!

Each record thereafter I put together in a different way, and these eventually enabled me to ascertain Pivotal Points and in turn demonstrate how to use them profitably marketwise. I have changed my calculations since then a number of times, but these records today are set up in such a way that they can talk to you also—if you but let them.

When a speculator can determine the Pivotal Point of a stock and interpret the action at that point, he may make a commitment with the positive assurance of being right from the start.

Many years ago I began profiting from the simplest type of Pivotal Point trades. Frequently I had observed that when a stock sold at 50, 100, 200 and even 300, a fast and straight movement almost invariably occurred after such points were passed.

My first attempt to profit on these Pivotal Points was in the old Anaconda stock. The instant it sold at 100, I placed an order to buy 4,000 shares. The order was not completed until the stock crossed 105 a few minutes later. That day it sold up about ten points more and the next day had another remarkable bulge. With only a few normal reactions of seven or eight points the advance continued to well over 150 in a short period of time. At no time was the Pivotal Point of 100 in danger.

From then on I rarely missed a big play where there was a Pivotal Point on which to work. When Anaconda sold at 200, I repeated my successful play and did the same thing again when it sold at 300. But on that occasion it did not carry through to the proper extent. It sold only to 302¾. Plainly it was flashing the danger signal. So I sold out my 8,000 shares, being fortunate enough to receive 300 a share for 5,000 shares and 299¾ for 1,500 shares. The 6,500 shares were sold in less than two minutes. But it took twenty-five minutes more to sell the remaining 1,500 shares in 100 and 200 lots down to 298¾, where the stock closed. I felt confident that if the stock broke below 300, it would have a swift downward move. Next morning there was excitement. Anaconda was way down in London, opened in New York substantially lower, and within a few days was selling at 225.

Bear in mind when using Pivotal Points in anticipating market movements, that if the stock does not perform as it should, after crossing the Pivotal Point, this is a danger signal which must be heeded.

As shown in the above incident, the action of Anaconda, after crossing 300, was entirely different than its action above 100 and 200, respectively. On those occasions there was a very fast advance of at least 10 to 15 points right after the Pivotal Point had been crossed. But this time, instead of the stock being hard to buy, the market was being supplied with quantities of it—to such an extent, the stock simply could not continue its advance. Therefore the action of the stock right above 300 clearly showed it had become a dangerous stock to own. It clearly showed that what usually happens when a stock crosses its Pivotal Point was not going to be the case this time.

On another occasion I recall waiting three weeks before starting to buy Bethlehem Steel. On April 7, 1915, it had reached its highest price on record: 87¾. Having observed that stocks passing a Pivotal Point gained rapidly, and being confident that Bethlehem Steel would go through 100, on April 8 I placed my first order to buy and accumulated my line from 99 up to 99¾. The same day the stock sold up to a high of 117. It never halted in its upward flight except for minor reactions until April 13, or five days later, when it sold at a high of 155, a breath-taking rise. This again illustrates the rewards which go to the person who has the patience to wait for and take advantage of the Pivotal Points.

But I was not through with Bethlehem. I repeated the operation at the 200 point, at the 300 point, and again at the dizzy peak of 400. Nor had

I finished, for I had anticipated what would happen in a bear market, when the stock broke the Pivotal Points on the way down. I learned the main thing was to watch the follow-through. I found it was an easy matter to turn around and get out of a position, when vitality was lacking after a stock crossed the line.

Incidentally, every time I lost patience and failed to await the Pivotal Points and fiddled around for some easy profits in the meantime, I would lose money.

Since those days there have been various split-ups in shares of high-priced stocks and, accordingly, opportunities such as those I have just reviewed do not occur so often. Nevertheless, there are other ways by which one can determine Pivotal Points. For instance, let us say that a new stock has been listed in the last two or three years and its high was 20, or any other figure, and that such a price was made two or three years ago. If something favorable happens in connection with the company, and the stock starts upward, usually it is a safe play to buy the minute it touches a brand-new high.

A stock may be brought out at 50, 60 or 70 a share, sell off 20 points or so, and then hold between the high and low for a year or two. Then if it ever sells below the previous low, that stock is likely to be in for a tremendous drop. Why? Because something must have gone wrong with the affairs of the company.

By keeping stock price records and taking into consideration the time element, you will be able to find many Pivotal Points on which to make a commitment for a fast movement. But to educate yourself to trade on these points requires patience. You must devote time to the study of records, made and entered in the record-book only by yourself, and in making notes at which prices the Pivotal

Points will be reached.

Fascinating almost beyond belief, the study of Pivotal Points is, you will find, a golden field for personal research. You will derive from successful trades based on your own judgment a singular pleasure and satisfaction. You will discover that profits made in this way are immensely more gratifying than any which could possibly come from the tips or guidance of someone else. If you make your own discovery, trade your own way, exercise patience, watch for the danger signals, you will develop a proper trend of thinking.

In the last chapters of this book I explain in detail my own method of determining the more complex Pivotal Points in conjunction with the Livermore Market Method.

Few people ever make money by trading on the occasional tips or recommendations of others. Many beg for information and then don't know how to use it.

At a dinner party one night a lady kept pestering me beyond endurance for some market advice. In one of those weak moments I told her to buy some Cerro de Pasco which that day had crossed a Pivotal Point. From the next morning's opening the stock advanced 15 points during the next week with only trifling reactions. Then the action of the stock gave forth a danger signal. I recalled the lady's inquiry and hastened to have Mrs. Livermore telephone her to sell. Fancy my surprise to learn that she had not yet bought the stock as she first wanted to see whether my information was correct. So wags the world of market tips.

Commodities frequently offer attractive Pivotal Points. Cocoa is traded in on the New York Cocoa Exchange. During most years the movements in this commodity do not offer many speculative inducements. Nevertheless, in making speculation a business, one automatically keeps an eye on all markets for the big opportunities.

During the year 1934 the high price of the December option in Cocoa was made in February at 6.23, the low was made in October at 4.28. In 1935 the high price was made in February at 5.74, the low in June at 4.54. The low price in 1936 was made in March at 5.13. But in August of that year for some reason the Cocoa market became a very different market. Great activity developed. When Cocoa sold that month at a price of 6.88, it was far beyond the highest price of the previous two years and above its last two Pivotal Points.

In September it sold at a high of 7.51; in October the high was 8.70; in November it was 10.80; in December 11.40; and in January 1937 it made an extreme high of 12.86, having recorded a rise of 600 points in a period of five months with only a few minor normal reactions.

Obviously there was a very good reason for this rapid rise, as only normal movements occur year in and year out. The reason was a severe shortage in the supply of Cocoa. Those closely watching Pivotal Points found a splendid opportunity in the Cocoa market.

It is when you set down prices in your record book and observe the patterns that the prices begin to talk to you. All of a sudden you realize that the picture you are making is acquiring a certain form. It is striving to make clear a situation that is building up. It suggests that you go back over your records and see what the last movement of importance was under a similar set of conditions. It is telling you that by careful analysis and good judgment you will be able to form an opinion. The price pattern reminds you that every movement of importance is but a repetition of similar price movements, that just as soon as you familiarize yourself with the actions of the past, you will be able to anticipate and act correctly and profitably upon forthcoming movements.

I want to emphasize the fact that I do not consider these records perfection, except as they serve me. I do know a basis is there for anticipating future movements and if anyone will study these records, keeping them themselves, they cannot fail to profit by it in their operations.

It would not surprise me if the persons who in the future follow my methods of keeping these records get even more out of them than I have. This statement is based on the premise that, whereas I arrived at my conclusions some time ago, as a result of my record analysis, those beginning to apply this method may very readily discover new points of value that I have missed. I would further clarify this by stating that I have not looked for any further points, because, applying it as I have for some time past, it has entirely served my personal purpose. Someone else, however, may develop from this basic method new ideas which, when applied, will enhance the value of my basic method for their purpose.

If they are able to do so, you may rest assured that I will not be jealous of their success!

VI

THE MILLION DOLLAR BLUNDER

IT is my purpose in these chapters to lay down some general trading principles. Later on there will be specific explanation of my formula for combining time element and price.

In consideration of these general trading principles it should be said that too many speculators buy or sell impulsively, acquiring their entire line at almost one price. That is wrong and dangerous.

Let us suppose that you want to buy 500 shares of a stock. Start by buying 100 shares. Then if the market advances buy another 100 shares and so on. But each succeeding purchase must be at a higher price than the previous one.

That same rule should be applied in selling short. Never make an additional sale unless it is at a lower price than the previous sale. By following this rule you will come nearer being on the right side than by any other method with which I am familiar. The reason for this procedure is that your trades have at all times shown you a profit. The fact that your trades do show you a profit is proof you are right.

Under my trading practice you first would size up the situation in regard to a particular stock. Next it is important to determine at what price you should allow yourself to enter the market. Study your book of price records, study carefully the movements of the past few weeks. When your chosen stock reaches the point you had previously decided it should reach if the move is going to start in earnest, that is the time to make your first commitment.

Having made that commitment, decide definitely the amount of money you are willing to risk should your calculations be wrong. You may make one or two commitments on this theory and lose. But by being consistent and never failing to re-enter the market again whenever your Pivotal Point is reached, you cannot help but be in when the real move does occur. You simply cannot be out of it.

But careful timing is essential . . . impatience costly.

Let me tell you how I once missed a million dollar profit through impatience and careless timing. I almost want to turn my face away in embarrassment when I tell this.

Many years ago I became strongly bullish on Cotton. I had formed a definite opinion that Cotton was in for a big rise. But as frequently happens the market itself was not ready to start. No sooner had I reached my conclusion, however, than I had to poke my nose into Cotton.

My initial play was for 20,000 bales, purchased at the market. This order ran the dull market up fifteen points. Then, after my last 100 bales had been bought, the market proceeded to slip back in twenty-four hours to the price at which it had been selling when I started buying. There it slept for a number of days. Finally, in disgust, I sold out, taking a loss of around $30,000, including commissions. Naturally my last 100 bales were sold at the lowest price of the reaction.

A few days later the market appealed to me again. I could not dismiss it from my mind, nor could I revise my original belief that it was in for a big move. So I re-bought my 20,000 bales. The same thing happened. Up jumped the market on my buying order and, after that, right back down it came with a thud. Waiting irked me, so once more I sold my holdings, the last lot at the lowest price again.

This costly operation I repeated five times in six weeks, losing on each operation between $25,000 to $30,000. I became disgusted with myself. Here I had chipped away almost $200,000 with not even a semblance of satisfaction. So I gave my manager an order to have the Cotton ticker removed before my arrival next morning. I did not want to be tempted to look at the Cotton market any more. It was too depressing, a mood not conducive to the clear thinking which is required at all times in the field of speculation.

And what happened? Two days after I had the ticker removed and had lost all interest in Cotton, the market started up, and it never stopped until it had risen 500 points. In that remarkable rise it had but one reaction as great as 40 points.

I had thus lost one of the most attractive and soundest plays I had ever figured out. There were two basic reasons. First, I lacked the patience to wait until the psychological time had arrived, pricewise, to begin my operation. I had known that if Cotton ever sold up to 12½ cents a pound it would be on its way to much higher prices. But no, I did not have the will power to wait. I thought I must make a few extra dollars quickly, before Cotton reached the buying point, and I acted before the market was ripe. Not only did I lose around $200,000 in actual money, but a profit of $1,000,000. For my original plan, well fixed in mind, contemplated the accumulation of 100,000 bales after the Pivotal Point had been passed. I could not have missed making a profit of 200 points or more on that move.

Secondly, to allow myself to become angry and disgusted with the Cotton market just because I had used bad judgment was not consistent with good speculative procedure. My loss was due wholly to lack of patience in awaiting the proper time to back up a preconceived opinion and plan.

I have long since learned, as all should learn, not to make excuses when wrong. Just admit it and try to profit by it. We all know when we are wrong. The market will tell the speculator when he is wrong, because he is losing money. When he first realizes he is wrong is the time to clear out, take his losses, try to keep smiling, study the record to determine the cause of his error, and await the next big opportunity. It is the net result over a period of time in which he is interested.

This sense of knowing when you are wrong even before the market tells you becomes, in time, rather highly developed. It is a subconscious tip-off. It is a signal from within that is based on knowledge of past market performances. Sometimes it is an advance agent of the trading formula. Let me explain more fully.

During the big Bull Market in the late twenties, there were times when I owned fairly large amounts of different stocks, which I held for a considerable period of time. During this period I never felt uneasy over my position whenever Natural Reactions occurred from time to time.

But sooner or later there would be a time when, after the market closed, I would become restive. That night I would find sound sleep difficult. Something would jog me into consciousness and I would awaken and begin thinking about the market. Next morning I would be afraid, almost, to look at the newspapers. Something sinister would seem impending. But perhaps I would find everything rosy and my strange feelings apparently unjustified. The market might open higher. Its action would be perfect. It would be right at the peak of its movement. One could almost laugh at his restless night. But I have learned to suppress such laughter.

For next day the story would be strikingly different. No disastrous news, but simply one of those sudden market turning points after a prolonged movement in one direction. On that day I would be genuinely disturbed. I would be faced with the rapid liquidation of a large line. The day before, I could have liquidated my entire position within two points of the extreme movement. But today, what a vast difference.

I believe many operators have had similar experiences with that curious inner mind which frequently flashes the danger signal when everything marketwise is aglow with hope. It is just one of those peculiar quirks that develops from long study and association with the market.

Frankly, I am always suspicious of the inner mind tip-off and usually prefer to apply the cold scientific formula. But the fact remains that on many occasions I have benefited to a high degree by giving attention to a feeling of great uneasiness at a time when I seemed to be sailing smooth seas.

This curious sidelight on trading is interesting because the feeling of danger ahead seems to be pronounced only among those sensitive to market action, those whose thoughts have followed a scientific pattern in seeking to determine price movements. To the rank and file of persons who speculate the bullish or bearish feeling is simply based on something overheard or some published comment.

Bear in mind that of the millions who speculate in all markets only a few devote their entire time to speculation. With an overwhelming majority it is only a hit-and-miss affair, and a costly one. Even among intelligent business and professional men and retired men it is a sideline to which they give small attention. Most of them would not be trading in stocks if at some time a good tip had not been passed along by a broker or customers' man.

Now and then someone begins trading because he has a hot inside tip from a friend in the inner councils of a large corporation. Let me here relate a hypothetical case.

You meet your corporation friend at luncheon or at a dinner party. You talk general business for a time. Then you ask about Great Shakes Corporation. Well, business is fine. It is just turning the corner and the future outlook is brilliant. Yes, the stock is attractive at this time.

"A very good buy, indeed," he will say and perhaps in all sincerity. "Our earnings are going to be excellent, in fact better than for a number of years past. Of course you recall, Jim, what the stock sold for the last time we had a boom."

You are enthused and lose little time in acquiring shares.

Each statement shows better business than during the last quarter. Extra dividends are declared. The stock moves up and up. And you drift into pleasant paper profit dreams. But in the course of time the company's business begins slipping dreadfully. You are not apprised of the fact. You only know the price of the stock has tobogganed. You hasten to call your friend.

"Yes," he will say, "the stock has had quite a break. But it seems to be only temporary. Volume of business is down somewhat. Having learned that fact the bears are attacking the stock. It's mostly short selling."

He may follow along with a lot of other platitudes, concealing the true reason. For he and his associates doubtless own a lot of the stock and have been selling as much and as rapidly as the market would take it since those first definite signs of a serious slump in their business appeared. To tell you the truth would simply invite your competition and perhaps the competition of your mutual friends in his selling campaign. It becomes almost a case of self-preservation.

So it is plain to see why your friend, the industrialist on the inside, can easily tell you when to buy. But he cannot and will not tell you when to sell. That would be equivalent almost to treason to his associates.

I urge you always to keep a little notebook with you. Jot down interesting market information: thoughts that may be helpful in the future; ideas that may be re-read from time to time; little personal observations you have made on price movements. On the first page of this little book I suggest you write—no, better print—it in ink:

> "Beware of inside information. . .
> *all* inside information."

It cannot be said too often that in speculation and investment, success comes only to those who work for it. No one is going to hand you a lot of easy money. It is like the story of the penniless tramp. His hunger gave him the audacity to enter a restaurant and order "a big, luscious, thick, juicy steak," and, he added to the colored waiter, "tell your boss to make it snappy." In a moment the waiter ambled back and whined: "De boss say if he had dat steak here he'd eat it hisself."

And if there was any easy money lying around, no one would be forcing it into your pocket.

VII

THE THREE MILLION DOLLAR PROFIT

IN the preceding chapter, I related how by not exercising patience I missed being in on a play that would have netted a handsome profit. Now I shall describe an instance where I bided my time and the result of waiting for the psychological moment.

In the summer of 1924, Wheat had reached a price that I term a Pivotal Point, so I stepped in with an initial buy order for five million bushels. At that time the Wheat market was an extremely large one, so that the execution of an order of this size had no appreciable effect on the price. Let me here indicate that a similar order given in a single stock would have been the equivalent of 50,000 shares.

Immediately after the execution of this order the market became dull for a few days, but it never declined below the Pivotal Point. The market then started up again and went a few cents higher than on the previous move, from which point it had a Natural Reaction and remained dull for a few days after which it resumed its advance.

As soon as it pierced the next Pivotal Point, I gave an order to buy another five million bushels. This was executed at an average price of 1½ cents above the Pivotal Point, which clearly indicated to me that the market was working itself into a strong position. Why? Because it was much more difficult to accumulate the second five million bushels than the first.

The ensuing day, instead of the market reacting as it had after the first order, it advanced 3 cents, which is exactly what it should have done if my analysis of the market was correct. From then on there developed what might be termed a real Bull Market. By that I mean an extensive movement had begun which I calculated would extend over a period of several months. I did not, however, fully realize the full possibilities which lay ahead. Then, when I had a 25 cents per bushel profit, I cashed in—and sat back and saw the market advance 20 cents more within a few days.

Right then I realized I had made a great mistake. Why had I been afraid of losing something I never really had? I was altogether too anxious to convert a paper profit into actual cash, when I should have been patient and had the courage to play the deal out to the end. I knew that in due time, when the upward trend had reached its Pivotal Point, I would be given a danger signal in ample time.

I therefore decided to re-enter the market and went back at an average of 25 cents higher than that at which I had sold my first commitment. At first I had only the courage to make one commitment, which represented 50% of what I had originally sold out. However, from there on I stayed with it until the danger signal gave warning.

On January 28, 1925, May Wheat sold at the high price of $2.05⅞ per bushel. On February 11 it had reacted to $1.77½.

During all this phenomenal advance in Wheat, there was another commodity, Rye, which had had an even more spectacular advance than Wheat.

However, the Rye market is a very small one compared to Wheat, so that the execution of a comparatively small order to buy would create a decidedly rapid advance.

During the above-described operations, I frequently had a large personal commitment in the market, and there were others who had equally as large commitments. One other operator was reputed to have accumulated a line of several million bushels of futures, in addition to many millions of bushels of cash wheat, and in order to help his position in Wheat to have also accumulated large amounts of cash Rye. He was also reputed to have used the Rye market at times when Wheat began to waver by placing orders to buy Rye.

As stated, the Rye market being small and narrow in comparison, the execution of any sizeable buying order immediately caused a rapid advance, and its reflection on Wheat prices was necessarily very marked. Whenever this method was used the public would rush in to buy Wheat, with the result that that commodity sold into new high territory.

This procedure went on successfully until the major movement reached its end. During the time Wheat was having its reaction Rye reacted in a corresponding way, declining from its high price made on January 28, 1925, of $1.82¼ cents, to a price of $1.54, being a reaction of 28¼ cents against a reaction of 28⅜ cents in Wheat. On March 2, May Wheat had recovered to within 3⅞ cents of its previous high, selling at $2.02, but Rye did not recover its decline in the same vigorous way as Wheat had, only being able to make a price of $1.70⅛, which was 12⅛ points below its previous high price.

Watching the market closely, as I was at that time, I was struck forcibly by the fact that something was wrong, since, during all the big Bull

Market, Rye had inevitably preceded the advance in Wheat. Now, instead of becoming a leader of the Grain Pit in its advance, it was lagging. Wheat had already recovered most of its entire abnormal reaction, whereas Rye failed to do so by about 12 cents per bushel. This action was something entirely new.

So I set to work analyzing, with a view to ascertaining the reason why Rye was not participating in the recovery proportionately to Wheat. The reason soon became evident. The public had a great interest in the Wheat market but none in Rye. If that was a one-man market, why, all of a sudden, was he neglecting it? I concluded that he either had no more interest in Rye and was out, or was so heavily involved in both markets that he was no longer in a position to make further commitments.

I decided then and there that it made no difference whether he was in or out of Rye—that eventually the result would be the same marketwise, so I put my theory to test.

The last quotation on Rye was $1.69¾ bid, and having determined to find out the real position in Rye, I gave an order to sell 200,000 bushels "at the market." When I placed that order Wheat was quoted at $2.02. Before the order was executed Rye had sold off 3 cents per bushel, and two minutes after the order was filled it was back at $1.68¾.

I discovered by the execution of that order that there were not many orders under the market. However, I was not yet certain what might develop after, so I gave an order to sell another 200,000 bushels, with the same result—down it went 3 cents before the order was executed, but after the execution it only rallied 1 cent against the 2 cents previously.

I still entertained some doubt as to the correctness of my analysis of the position of the market, so I gave a third order to sell 200,000 bushels, with the same result—the market again went down, but this time there was no rally. It kept on going down on its own momentum.

That was the tip-off for which I was watching and waiting. If someone held a big position in the Wheat market and did not for some reason or other protect the Rye market (and what his reason was did not concern me), I felt confident that he would not or could not support the Wheat market. So I immediately gave an order to sell 5,000,000 bushels of May Wheat "at the market." It was sold from $2.01 to $1.99. That night it closed around $1.97 and Rye at $1.65. I was glad the last part of my order was completed below $2.00 because the $2.00 price was a Pivotal Point, and the market having broken through that Pivotal Point, I felt sure of my position. Naturally I never had any worries about that trade.

A few days later I bought my Rye in, which I had sold only as a testing operation to ascertain the position of the Wheat market, and chalked up a profit of $250,000.00 on the transaction.

In the meantime, I kept on selling Wheat until I had accumulated a short line of fifteen million bushels. March 16, May Wheat closed at $1.64½, and the next morning Liverpool was 3 cents lower than due, which on a parity basis should cause our market to open around $1.61.

Then I did something that experience taught me I should not do, namely, give an order at a specified price before the market opened. But temptation submerged my better judgment and I gave an order to buy five million bushels at $1.61, which was 3½ cents below the previous night's close. The opening showed a price range of $1.61 to $1.54. Thereupon I said to myself: "It serves you right for breaking a rule you know you should not have broken." But again it was a case of human instinct overcoming innate judgment. I would have bet anything that my order would be executed at the stipulated price of $1.61, which was the high of the opening price range.

Accordingly, when I saw the price of $1.54, I gave another order to buy five million bushels. Immediately thereafter I received a report: "Bought five million bushels May Wheat at $1.53."

Again I entered my order for another five million bushels. In less than one minute the report came; "Bought five million bushels at $1.53," which I naturally assumed was the price at which my third order had been filled. I then asked for a report on my first order. The following was handed to me:

"The first five million bushels reported to you filled your first order.

"The second five million bushels reported covered your second order.

"Here is the report on your third order:
      "3½ million bushels at 153
      "1   "   "   " 153⅛
      "500,000   "   " 153¼"

The low price that day was $1.51 and next day Wheat was back to $1.64. That was the first time in my experience I had ever received an execution on a limited order of that nature. I had given an order to buy five million bushels at $1.61—the market opened at my bid price of $1.61 to 7 cents lower, $1.54, which represented a difference of $350,000.00.

A short time later I had occasion to be in Chicago, and asked the man who was in charge of placing my orders how it happened that I received such excellent execution of my first limited order. He informed me that he happened to know there was an order in the market to sell thirty-five million bushels "at the market." That being the case, he realized that no matter how low the market might open there would be plenty of Wheat for sale at the lower opening price after the opening, so he merely waited until the opening range and then put in my order "at the market."

He stated that had it not been for my orders reaching the Pit as they did, the market would have had a tremendous break from the opening level.

The final net result of these transactions showed a profit of over $3,000,000.00.

This illustrates the value of having a short interest in speculative markets because the short interests become willing buyers, and those willing buyers act as a much-needed stabilizer in times of panic.

Today operations of this kind are not possible, as the Commodities Exchange Administration limits the size of any one individual's position in the grain market to two million bushels, and while there has been no limit placed on the size of anyone's commitment in the stock market, it is equally impossible for any one operator to establish a sizeable short position under the existing rules in respect to selling short.

I therefore believe the day of the old speculator has gone. His place will be taken in the future by the semi-investor, who, while not able to make such large sums in the market quickly, will be able to make more money over a given period and be able to keep it. I hold the firm belief that the future successful semi-investor will only operate at the psychological time and will eventually realize a much larger percentage out of every minor or major movement than the purely speculative-minded operator ever did.

VIII

THE LIVERMORE MARKET KEY

MANY years of my life had been devoted to speculation before it dawned upon me that nothing new was happening in the stock market, that price movements were simply being repeated, that while there was variation in different stocks the general price pattern was the same.

The urge fell upon me, as I have said, to keep price records that might be a guide to price movements. This I undertook with some zest. Then I began striving to find a point to start from in helping me to anticipate future movements. That was no easy task.

Now I can look back on those initial efforts and understand why they were not immediately fruitful. Having then a purely speculative mind, I was trying to devise a policy for trading in and out of the market all the time, catching the small intermediate moves. This was wrong, and in time I clearly recognized the fact.

I continued keeping my records, confident that they had a genuine value which only awaited my discovery. At length the secret unfolded. The records told me plainly that they would do nothing for me in the way of intermediate movements. But if I would but use my eyes, I would see the formation of patterms that would foretell major movements.

Right then I determined to eliminate all the minor movements.

By continued close study of the many records I had kept the realization struck me that the *time element* was vital in forming a correct opinion as to the approach of the really important movements. With renewed vigor I concentrated on that feature. What I wanted to discover was a method of recognizing what constituted the minor swings. I realized a market in a definite trend still had numerous intermediate oscillations. They had been confusing. They were no longer to be my concern.

I wanted to find out what constituted the beginning of a Natural Reaction or a Natural Rally. So I began checking the distances of price movements. First I based my calculations on one point. That was no good. Then two points, and so on, until finally I arrived at a point that represented what I thought should constitute the beginning of a Natural Reaction or Natural Rally.

To simplify the picture I had printed a special sheet of paper, ruled in distinctive columns, and so arranged as to give me what I term my Map for Anticipating Future Movements. For each stock I use six columns. Prices are recorded in the columns as they occur. Each column has its heading.

First column is headed Secondary Rally.
Second is headed Natural Rally.
Third is headed Upward Trend.
Fourth is headed Downward Trend.
Fifth is headed Natural Reaction.
Sixth is headed Secondary Reaction.

When figures are recorded in the Upward Trend column they are entered in black ink. In the next two columns to the left I insert the figures in pencil. When figures are recorded in the Downward Trend column they are entered in red ink, and in

the next two columns to the right, the entries are
also made in pencil.

Thus when recording the prices either in the Upward Trend column or in the Downward Trend
column I am impressed with the actual trend at
the time. Those figures in distinctive ink talk to
me. The red ink or the black ink, used persistently,
tells a story that is unmistakable.

When the pencil remains in use I realize I am
simply noting the natural oscillations. (In the reproduction of my records later on, bear in mind
that the prices entered in light blue ink are those
for which I use a pencil on my sheets).

I decided a stock selling around $30.00 or higher
would have to rally or react from an extreme point
to the extent of approximately six points before I
could recognize that a Natural Rally or Natural
Reaction was in the making. This rally or reaction
does not indicate that the trend of the market has
changed its course. It simply indicates that the
market is experiencing a natural movement. The
trend is exactly the same as it was before the rally
or reaction occurred.

I would here explain that I do not take the action of a single stock as an indication that the trend
has been positively changed for that group. Instead
I take the combined action of two stocks in any
group before I recognize the trend has definitely
changed, hence the Key Price. By combining the
prices and movements in these two stocks I arrive
at what I call my Key Price. I find that an individual stock sometimes has a movement big enough to
put it in my Upward Trend column or my Downward Trend column. But there is danger of being
caught in a false movement by depending upon
only one stock. The movement of the two stocks
combined gives reasonable assurance. Thus, a positive change of the trend must be confirmed by the

action of the Key Price.

Let me illustrate this Key Price method. Strictly adhering to the six-point movement to be used as a basis, you will note in my subsequent records that at times I record a price in U.S. Steel if it only has had a move, let us say, of 5⅛ points because you will find a corresponding movement in Bethlehem Steel, say, of 7 points. Taken together the price movements of the two stocks constitute the Key Price. This Key Price, then, totals twelve points or better, the proper distance required.

When a recording point has been reached—that is, a move of six points average by each of the two stocks—I continue to set down in that same column the extreme price made any day, whenever it is higher than the last price recorded in the Upward Trend column or is lower than the last price recorded in the Downward Trend column. This goes on until a reverse movement starts. This later movement in the other direction will, of course, be based on the same six points average, or twelve points for the Key Price.

You will notice that from then on I never deviate from those points. I make no exceptions. Nor do I make excuses, if the results are not exactly as I anticipated. Remember, these prices I set forth in my records are not my prices. These points have been determined by actual prices registered in the day's trading.

It would be presumptuous for me to say I had arrived at the exact point from which my record of prices should start. It would also be misleading and insincere. I can only say that after years of checking and observation I feel I have arrived somewhere near a point that can be used as a basis for keeping records. From these records one can visualize a map useful in determining the approach of important price movements.

Someone has said that success rides upon the hour of decision.

Certainly success with this plan depends upon courage to act and act promptly when your records tell you to do so. There is no place for vacillation. You must train your mind along those lines. If you are going to wait upon someone else for explanations or reasons or reassurances, the time for action will have escaped.

To give an illustration: After the rapid advance all stocks had following the declaration of war in Europe, a Natural Reaction occurred in the whole market. Then all the stocks in the four prominent groups recovered their reaction and all sold at new high prices—with the exception of the stocks in the Steel group. Anyone keeping records according to my method would have had their attention drawn very forcefully to the action of the Steel stocks. Now there must have been a very good reason why the Steel stocks refused to continue their advance along with the other groups. There was a good reason! But at the time I did not know it, and I doubt very much that anyone could have given a valid explanation for it. However, anyone who had been recording prices would have realized by the action of the Steel stocks that the upward movement in the Steel group had ended. It was not until the middle of January 1940, four months later, that the public was given the facts and the action of the Steel stocks was explained. An announcement was made that during that time the English Government had disposed of over 100,000 shares of U.S. Steel, and in addition Canada had sold 20,000 shares. When that announcement was made the price of U.S. Steel was 26 points lower than its high price attained in September 1939 and Bethlehem Steel was 29 points lower, whereas the prices of the other three prominent groups were off only

2½ to 12¾ points from the high prices that were made at the same time the Steels made their highs. This incident proves the folly of trying to find out "a good reason" why you should buy or sell a given stock. If you wait until you have the reason given you, you will have missed the opportunity of having acted at the proper time! The only reason an investor or speculator should ever want to have pointed out to him is the action of the market itself. Whenever the market does not act right or in the way it should—that is reason enough for you to change your opinion and change it immediately. Remember: there is always a reason for a stock acting the way it does. But also remember: the chances are that you will not become acquainted with that reason until some time in the future, when it is too late to act on it profitably.

I repeat that the formula does not provide points whereby you can make additional trades, with assurance, on intermediate fluctuations which occur during a major move. *The intent is to catch the major moves*, to indicate the beginning and the end of movements of *importance*. And for such purpose you will find the formula of singular value if faithfully pursued. It should, perhaps, also be repeated that this formula is designed for active stocks selling above an approximate price of 30. While the same basic principles are of course operative in anticipating the market action of all stocks, certain adjustments in the formula must be made in considering the very low-priced issues.

There is nothing complicated about it. The various phases will be absorbed quickly and with easy understanding by those who are interested.

In the next chapter is given the exact reproduction of my records, with full explanation of the figures which I have entered.

IX

EXPLANATORY RULES

1   Record prices in Upward Trend Column
        in black ink.

2   Record prices in Downward Trend column
        in red ink.

3   Record prices in the other four columns in
        pencil.

4 (a)   Draw red lines under your last recorded
        price in the Upward Trend column the first
        day you start to record figures in the Natu-
        ral Reaction column. You begin to do this
        on the first reaction of approximately six
        points from the last price recorded in the
        Upward Trend column.

  (b)   Draw red lines under your last recorded
        price in the Natural Reaction column the
        first day you start to record figures in the
        Natural Rally column or in the Upward
        Trend column. You begin to do this on the
        first rally of approximately six points from
        the last price recorded in the Natural Re-
        action column.

        *You now have two Pivotal Points to watch,
        and depending on how prices are recorded*

when the market returns to around one of those points, you will then be able to form an opinion as to whether the positive trend is going to be resumed in earnest—or whether the movement has ended.

(c) Draw black lines under your last recorded price in the Downward Trend column the first day you start to record figures in the Natural Rally column. You begin to do this on the first rally of approximately six points from the last price recorded in the Downward Trend column.

(d) Draw black lines under your last recorded price in the Natural Rally column the first day you start to record figures in the Natural Reaction column or in the Downward Trend column. You begin to do this on the first reaction of approximately six points from the last price recorded in the Natural Rally column.

5 (a) When recording in the Natural Rally column and a price is reached that is three or more points *above* the last price recorded in the Natural Rally column (with black lines underneath), then that price should be entered in black ink in the Upward Trend column.

(b) When recording in the Natural Reaction column and a price is reached that is three or more points *below* the last price recorded in the Natural Reaction column (with red lines underneath), then that price should be entered in red ink in the Downward Trend column.

6 (a) When a reaction occurs to an extent of approximately six points, after you have been recording prices in the Upward Trend column, you then start to record those prices in the Natural Reaction column, and continue to do so every day thereafter that the stock sells at a price which is lower than the last recorded price in the Natural Reaction column.

(b) When a reaction occurs to an extent of approximately six points, after you have been recording prices in the Natural Rally column, you then start to record those prices in the Natural Reaction column, and continue to do so every day thereafter that the stock sells at a price which is lower than the last recorded price in the Natural Reaction column. In case a price is made which is lower than the last recorded price in the Downward Trend column, you would then record that price in the Downward Trend column.

(c) When a rally occurs to an extent of approximately six points, after you have been recording prices in the Downward Trend column, you then start to record those prices in the Natural Rally column, and continue to do so every day thereafter that the stock sells at a price which is higher than the last recorded price in the Natural Rally column.

(d) When a rally occurs to an extent of approximately six points, after you have been recording prices in the Natural Reaction column, you then start to record those prices in the Natural Rally column, and continue to do so every day thereafter that the stock sells at a price which is higher than the last recorded price in the Natural Rally column. In case a price is made which is higher than the last recorded price in the Upward Trend column, you would then record that price in the Upward Trend column.

(e) When you start to record figures in the Natural Reaction column and a price is reached *that is lower than the last recorded figure in the Downward Trend column*— then that price should be entered in red ink in the Downward Trend column.

(f) The same rule applies when you are recording figures in the Natural Rally column and a price is reached *that is higher than the last price recorded in the Upward Trend column*—then you would cease recording in the Natural Rally column and record that price in black ink in the Upward Trend column.

(g) In case you had been recording in the Natural Reaction column and a rally should occur of approximately six points from the last recorded figure in the Natural Reaction column—but that price did not exceed the last price recorded in the Natural Rally column—that price should be recorded in the *Secondary* Rally column and should continue to be so recorded until a price had been made which exceeded the last figure recorded in the Natural Rally column. When that occurs, you should commence to record prices in the Naturally Rally column once again.

(h) In case you have been recording in the Natural Rally column and a reaction should occur of approximately six points, but the price reached on that reaction was *not lower* than the last recorded figure in your *Natural* Reaction column—that price should be entered in your *Secondary* Reaction column, and you should continue to record prices in that column until a price was made that was *lower* than the last price recorded in the Natural Reaction column. When that occurs, you should commence to record prices in the Natural Reaction column once again.

7 The same rules apply when recording the Key Price—except that you use twelve points as a basis instead of six points used in individual stocks.

8 The last price recorded in the Downward or Upward Trend columns becomes a Pivotal Point as soon as you begin to record prices in the Natural Rally or Natural Reaction columns. After a rally or reaction has ended you start to record again in the reverse column, and the extreme price made in the previous column then becomes another Pivotal Point.

It is after two Pivotal Point have been reached that these records become of great value to you in helping you anticipate correctly the next movement of importance. These Pivotal Points are drawn to your attention by having a double line drawn underneath them in either red ink or black ink. Those lines are drawn for the express purpose of keeping those points before you, and should be watched very carefully whenever prices are made and recorded near or at one of those points. Your decision to act will then depend on how prices are recorded from then on.

9 (a) When you see black lines drawn below the last recorded red-ink figure in the Downward Trend column—you *may* be given a signal to buy near that point.

(b) When black lines are drawn below a price recorded in the Natural Rally column, and if the stock on its next rally reaches a point near that Pivotal Point price, that is the time you are going to find out whether the market is strong enough definitely to change its course into the Upward Trend column.

(c) The reverse holds true when you see red lines drawn under the last price recorded in the Upward Trend column, and when red lines are drawn below the last price recorded in the Natural Reaction column.

10 (a) This whole method is designed to enable one to see clearly whether a stock is acting the way it ought to, after its first Natural Rally or Reaction has occurred. If the movement is going to be resumed in a positive manner—either up or down—it will carry through its previous Pivotal Point—in individual stocks by three points, or, in the Key Price by six points.

(b) If the stock fails to do this—and in a reaction sells three points or more *below* the last Pivotal Point (recorded in the Upward Trend column with red lines drawn underneath), it would indicate that the Upward Trend in the stock is over.

(c)　Applying the rule to the Downward Trend: Whenever, after a Natural Rally has ended, new prices are being recorded in the Downward Trend column, these new prices must extend three or more points *below* the last Pivotal Point (with black lines underneath), if the Downward Trend is to be positively resumed.

(d)　If the stock fails to do this, and on a rally sells three or more points *above* the last Pivotal Point (recorded in the Downward Trend column with black lines drawn underneath), it would indicate that the Downward Trend in the stock is over.

(e)　When recording in the Natural Rally column, if the rally ends a short distance below the last Pivotal Point in the Upward Trend column (with red lines underneath), and the stock reacts three or more points from that price, it is a danger signal, which would indicate the Upward Trend in that stock is over.

(f)　When recording in the Natural Reaction column, if the reaction ends a short distance above the last Pivotal Point in the Downward Trend column (with black lines underneath), and the stock rallies three or more points from that price, it is a danger signal, which would indicate the Downward Trend in that stock is over.

CHARTS AND EXPLANATIONS

FOR THE

LIVERMORE MARKET KEY

On April 2nd prices began to be recorded in Natural Rally column. Refer to Explanatory Rule 6-B. Draw black line under last price in Downward Trend column. Refer to Explanatory Rule 4-C.

On April 28th, prices began to be recorded in Natural Reaction column. Refer to Explanatory Rule 4-D.

CHART ONE

DATE	SECONDARY RALLY	NATURAL RALLY	UPWARD TREND	DOWNWARD TREND	NATURAL REACTION	SECONDARY REACTION	SECONDARY RALLY	NATURAL RALLY	UPWARD TREND	DOWNWARD TREND	NATURAL REACTION	SECONDARY REACTION	SECONDARY RALLY	NATURAL RALLY	UPWARD TREND	DOWNWARD TREND	NATURAL REACTION	SECONDARY REACTION
		$65\frac{3}{4}$						57						$122\frac{3}{4}$				
				$48\frac{1}{2}$							$43\frac{1}{4}$					$91\frac{3}{4}$		
		$62\frac{1}{8}$								$65\frac{7}{8}$				128				
				$48\frac{1}{4}$							$50\frac{1}{8}$						$98\frac{3}{8}$	
								$56\frac{7}{8}$										
1938																		
DATE				U.S. STEEL					BETHLEHEM STEEL						KEY PRICE			
MAR 23				47							$50\frac{1}{4}$						$97\frac{1}{4}$	
24																		
25				$44\frac{3}{4}$						$46\frac{3}{4}$						$91\frac{1}{2}$		
SAT 26				44						46						90		
28				$43\frac{5}{8}$												$89\frac{5}{8}$		
29				$39\frac{5}{8}$						43						$82\frac{5}{8}$		
30				39						$42\frac{1}{8}$						$81\frac{1}{8}$		
31				38						40						78		
APR. 1																		
SAT. 2		$43\frac{1}{2}$						$46\frac{3}{8}$						$89\frac{7}{8}$				
4																		
5																		
6																		
7																		
8																		
SAT. 9		$46\frac{1}{2}$						$49\frac{3}{4}$						$96\frac{1}{4}$				
11																		
12																		
13		$47\frac{1}{4}$												97				
14		$47\frac{1}{2}$												$97\frac{1}{4}$				
SAT. 16		49						52						101				
18																		
19																		
20																		
21																		
22																		
SAT. 23																		
25																		
26																		
27																		
28					43													
29					$42\frac{3}{8}$						45						$87\frac{3}{8}$	
SAT 30																		
MAY 2					$41\frac{1}{2}$						$44\frac{1}{4}$						$85\frac{3}{4}$	
3																		
4																		

All of these prices recorded are brought forth from the preceding page in order to keep the Pivotal Points always before you.

During the period from May 5th to May 21st inclusive, no prices were recorded because no prices were made lower than the last price recorded in the Natural Reaction column. Nor was there sufficient rally to be recorded.

On May 27th, the price of Bethlehem Steel was recorded in red because it was a lower price than the previous price recorded in the Downward Trend column. Refer to Explanatory Rule 6-C.

On June 2nd, Bethlehem Steel became a buy at 43. Refer to Explanatory Rule 10-C and D. On the same day U. S. Steel became a buy at 42¼. Refer to Explanatory Rule 10-F.

On June 10th, a price was recorded in the Secondary Rally column of Bethlehem Steel. Refer to Explanatory Rule 6-E.

	SECONDARY RALLY	NATURAL RALLY	UPWARD TREND	DOWNWARD TREND	NATURAL REACTION	SECONDARY REACTION	SECONDARY RALLY	NATURAL RALLY	UPWARD TREND	DOWNWARD TREND	NATURAL REACTION	SECONDARY REACTION	SECONDARY RALLY	NATURAL RALLY	UPWARD TREND	DOWNWARD TREND	NATURAL REACTION	SECONDARY REACTION
				<u>38</u>						<u>40</u>						<u>78</u>		
		49						52						101				
1938					41½						44¼						85¾	
DATE		U.S. STEEL						BETHLEHEM STEEL						KEY PRICE				
MAY 5																		
6																		
SAT. 7																		
9																		
10																		
11																		
12																		
13																		
SAT. 14																		
16																		
17																		
18																		
19																		
20																		
SAT. 21																		
23											44⅛							85⅝	
24											43½							85	
25					41⅜						42½							83⅞	
26					40⅛						40½							80⅝	
27					39⅞					39¾								79⅝	
SAT. 28																		
31					39¼													79	
JUNE 1																		
2																		
3																		
SAT. 4																		
6																		
7																		
8																		
9																		
10							46½											
SAT. 11																		
13																		
14																		
15																		
16																		

On June 20th, the price of U. S. Steel was recorded in the Secondary Rally column. Refer to Explanatory Rule 6-G.

On June 24th, prices of U. S. Steel and Bethlehem Steel were recorded in black ink in the Upward Trend column. Refer to Explanatory Rule 5-A.

On July 11th, prices of U.S. Steel and Bethlehem Steel were recorded in the Natural Reaction column. Refer to Explanatory Rules 6-A and 4-A.

On July 19th, prices of U.S. Steel and Bethlehem Steel were recorded in the Upward Trend column in black ink because those prices were higher than the last prices that were recorded in those columns. Refer to Explanatory Rule 4-B.

CHART THREE

Date	Secondary Rally	Natural Rally	Upward Trend	Downward Trend	Natural Reaction	Secondary Reaction	Secondary Rally	Natural Rally	Upward Trend	Downward Trend	Natural Reaction	Secondary Reaction	Secondary Rally	Natural Rally	Upward Trend	Downward Trend	Natural Reaction	Secondary Reaction
			38							40						78		
		49						52						101				
					$39\frac{1}{4}$						$39\frac{3}{4}$						79	
1938							$46\frac{1}{2}$											
DATE		U.S. STEEL							BETHLEHEM STEEL						KEY PRICE			
JUNE 17																		
SAT.18																		
20	$45\frac{3}{8}$						$48\frac{1}{4}$						$93\frac{5}{8}$					
21	$46\frac{1}{2}$						$49\frac{7}{8}$						$96\frac{3}{8}$					
22	$48\frac{1}{2}$						$50\frac{7}{8}$						$99\frac{3}{8}$					
23		$51\frac{1}{4}$						$53\frac{1}{4}$						$104\frac{1}{2}$				
24			$53\frac{3}{4}$						$55\frac{1}{8}$						$108\frac{7}{8}$			
SAT.25			$54\frac{7}{8}$						$58\frac{1}{8}$						113			
27																		
28																		
29			$56\frac{7}{8}$						$60\frac{1}{8}$						117			
30			$58\frac{3}{8}$						$61\frac{5}{8}$						120			
JULY 1			59												$120\frac{5}{8}$			
SAT.2			$60\frac{7}{8}$						$62\frac{1}{2}$						$123\frac{3}{8}$			
5																		
6																		
7			$61\frac{3}{4}$												$124\frac{1}{4}$			
8																		
SAT.9																		
11				$55\frac{5}{8}$						$56\frac{3}{4}$						$112\frac{3}{8}$		
12				$55\frac{1}{2}$												$112\frac{1}{4}$		
13																		
14																		
15																		
SAT.16																		
18																		
19			$62\frac{3}{8}$						$63\frac{1}{8}$						$125\frac{1}{2}$			
20																		
21																		
22																		
SAT.23																		
25			$63\frac{1}{4}$												$126\frac{3}{8}$			
26																		
27																		
28																		
29																		

On August 12th, the price of U. S. Steel was recorded in the Secondary Re-action column because the price was not lower than the last price previously recorded in the Natural Reaction column. On the same day the price of Bethlehem Steel was recorded in the Natural Reaction column because that price was lower than the last price previously recorded in the Natural Reaction column.

On August 24th, prices of U. S. Steel and Bethlehem Steel were recorded in the Natural Rally column. Refer to Explanatory Rule 6-D.

On August 29th, prices of U. S. Steel and Bethlehem Steel were recorded in the Secondary Reaction column. Refer to Explanatory Rule 6-H.

CHART FOUR

	SECONDARY RALLY	NATURAL RALLY	UPWARD TREND	DOWNWARD TREND	NATURAL REACTION	SECONDARY REACTION	SECONDARY RALLY	NATURAL RALLY	UPWARD TREND	DOWNWARD TREND	NATURAL REACTION	SECONDARY REACTION	SECONDARY RALLY	NATURAL RALLY	UPWARD TREND	DOWNWARD TREND	NATURAL REACTION	SECONDARY REACTION
			61 3/4						62 1/2						124 1/4			
				55 1/2							56 3/4						124	
			63 1/4						63 1/8						126 3/8			
1938			U.S. STEEL						BETHLEHEM STEEL						KEY PRICE			
DATE																		
SAT. JULY 30																		
AUG. 1																		
2																		
3																		
4																		
5																		
SAT. 6																		
8																		
9																		
10																		
11																		
12					56 5/8						54 7/8						111 1/2	
SAT. 13					56 1/2						54 5/8						111 1/8	
15																		
16																		
17																		
18																		
19																		
SAT. 20																		
22																		
23																		
24	61 5/8							61 3/8						123				
25																		
26	61 7/8							61 1/2						123 3/8				
SAT. 27																		
29					56 1/8							55					—	
30																		
31																		
SEPT. 1																		
2																		
SAT. 3																		
6																		
7																		
8																		
9																		
SAT. 10																		

On September 14th, the price of U. S. Steel was recorded in the Downward Trend column. Refer to Explanatory Rule 5-B. On the same day a price was recorded in the Natural Reaction column of Bethlehem Steel. That price was still being recorded in the Natural Reaction column because it had not reached a price that was 3 points lower than its previous price with red lines drawn. On September 20th, prices of U. S. Steel and Bethlehem Steel were recorded in the Natural Rally column. Refer to Explanatory Rule 6-C for U. S. Steel and 6-D for Bethlehem Steel.

On September 24th, the price of U. S. Steel was recorded in the Downward Trend column in red ink, being a new price in that column.

On September 29th, prices of U. S. Steel and Bethlehem Steel were recorded in the Secondary Rally column. Refer to Explanatory Rule 6-G.

On October 5th, the price of U. S. Steel was recorded in the Upward Trend column in black ink. Refer to Explanatory Rule 5-A.

On October 8th, the price of Bethlehem Steel was recorded in the Upward Trend column in black ink. Refer to Explanatory Rule 6-D.

CHART FIVE

	SECONDARY RALLY	NATURAL RALLY	UPWARD TREND	DOWNWARD TREND	NATURAL REACTION	SECONDARY REACTION	SECONDARY RALLY	NATURAL RALLY	UPWARD TREND	DOWNWARD TREND	NATURAL REACTION	SECONDARY REACTION	SECONDARY RALLY	NATURAL RALLY	UPWARD TREND	DOWNWARD TREND	NATURAL REACTION	SECONDARY REACTION
			63¼						63⅛						126⅝			
					55½						54⅜						111⅛	
								61½						123⅜				
		61⅞																
1938						56⅛						55						
DATE			U.S. STEEL						BETHLEHEM STEEL						KEY PRICE			
SEPT. 12																		
13					54¼						53⅝						107⅞	
14				52							52½					104½		
15																		
16																		
SAT. 17																		
19																		
20		57⅝						58¼										
21		58												116¼				
22																		
23																		
SAT. 24				51⅞							52					103⅞		
26				51⅛							51¼					102⅜		
27																		
28				50⅞							51					101⅞		
29	57⅛						57¾						114⅞					
30		59¼						59½						118¾				
SAT. OCT. 1		60¼						60						120¼				
3		60⅜						60⅜						120¾				
4																		
5			62					62							124			
6			63					63							126			
7																		
SAT. 8			64¼						64						128¼			
10																		
11																		
13			65⅜						65⅛						130½			
14																		
SAT. 15																		
17																		
18																		
19																		
20																		
21																		
SAT. 22			65⅞						67½						133⅜			
24			66												133½			

On November 18th, prices of U. S. Steel and Bethlehem Steel were recorded in the Natural Reaction column. Refer to Explanatory Rule 6-A.

CHART SIX

DATE	SECONDARY RALLY	NATURAL RALLY	UPWARD TREND	DOWNWARD TREND	NATURAL REACTION	SECONDARY REACTION	SECONDARY RALLY	NATURAL RALLY	UPWARD TREND	DOWNWARD TREND	NATURAL REACTION	SECONDARY REACTION	SECONDARY RALLY	NATURAL RALLY	UPWARD TREND	DOWNWARD TREND	NATURAL REACTION	SECONDARY REACTION
1938			66						$67\frac{1}{2}$						$133\frac{1}{2}$			
DATE		U.S. STEEL						BETHLEHEM STEEL						KEY PRICE				
OCT.25			$66\frac{1}{8}$						$67\frac{7}{8}$						134			
26																		
27			$66\frac{1}{2}$						$68\frac{7}{8}$						$135\frac{3}{8}$			
28																		
SAT.29																		
31																		
NOV.1									69						$135\frac{1}{2}$			
2																		
3									$69\frac{1}{2}$						136			
4																		
SAT.5																		
7			$66\frac{3}{4}$						$71\frac{7}{8}$						$138\frac{5}{8}$			
9			$69\frac{1}{2}$						$75\frac{3}{8}$						$144\frac{7}{8}$			
10			70						$75\frac{1}{2}$						$145\frac{1}{2}$			
SAT.12			$71\frac{1}{4}$						$77\frac{5}{8}$						$148\frac{7}{8}$			
14																		
15																		
16																		
17																		
18				$65\frac{1}{8}$						$71\frac{7}{8}$							137	
SAT.19																		
21																		
22																		
23																		
25																		
SAT.26				$63\frac{1}{4}$						$71\frac{1}{2}$							$134\frac{3}{4}$	
28				61						$68\frac{3}{4}$							$129\frac{3}{4}$	
29																		
30																		
DEC.1																		
2																		
SAT.3																		
5																		
6																		
7																		
8																		

On December 14th, prices of U. S. Steel and Bethlehem Steel were recorded in the Natural Rally column. Refer to Explanatory Rule 6-D.

On December 28th, the price of Bethlehem Steel was recorded in the Upward Trend column in black ink, being a price higher than the last price previously recorded in that column.

On January 4th, the next trend of the market was being indicated according to the Livermore method. Refer to Explanatory Rules 10-A and B.

On January 12th, prices of U. S. Steel and Bethlehem Steel were recorded in the Secondary Reaction column. Refer to Explanatory Rule 6-H.

CHART SEVEN

DATE	SECONDARY RALLY	NATURAL RALLY	UPWARD TREND	DOWNWARD TREND	NATURAL REACTION	SECONDARY REACTION	SECONDARY RALLY	NATURAL RALLY	UPWARD TREND	DOWNWARD TREND	NATURAL REACTION	SECONDARY REACTION	SECONDARY RALLY	NATURAL RALLY	UPWARD TREND	DOWNWARD TREND	NATURAL REACTION	SECONDARY REACTION
			$71\frac{1}{4}$						$77\frac{5}{8}$						$148\frac{7}{8}$			
					61						$68\frac{3}{4}$						$129\frac{3}{4}$	
1938			U.S. STEEL						BETHLEHEM STEEL						KEY PRICE			
DATE																		
DEC.9																		
SAT.10																		
12																		
13																		
14		$66\frac{5}{8}$						$75\frac{1}{4}$						$141\frac{7}{8}$				
15		$67\frac{1}{8}$						$76\frac{3}{8}$						$143\frac{1}{2}$				
16																		
SAT.17																		
19																		
20																		
21																		
22																		
23																		
SAT.24																		
27																		
28		$67\frac{3}{4}$						78						$145\frac{3}{4}$				
29																		
30																		
SAT.31 1939 JAN.3																		
4		70						80						150				
5																		
6																		
SAT.7																		
9																		
10																		
11									$73\frac{3}{4}$									
12					$62\frac{5}{8}$				$71\frac{1}{2}$									$139\frac{1}{8}$
13																		
SAT.14																		
16																		
17																		
18																		
19																		
20																		
SAT.21					62				$69\frac{1}{2}$									$131\frac{1}{2}$

On January 23rd, prices of U. S. Steel and Bethlehem Steel were recorded in the Downward Trend column. Refer to Explanatory Rule 5-B.

On January 31st, prices of U. S. Steel and Bethlehem Steel were recorded in the Natural Rally column. Refer to Explanatory Rules 6-C and 4-C.

Date	Secondary Rally	Natural Rally	Upward Trend	Downward Trend	Natural Reaction	Secondary Reaction	Secondary Rally	Natural Rally	Upward Trend	Downward Trend	Natural Reaction	Secondary Reaction	Secondary Rally	Natural Rally	Upward Trend	Downward Trend	Natural Reaction	Secondary Reaction
			71 1/4						77 5/8						148 7/8			
				61						68 3/4							129 3/4	
		70						80						150				
1939				62							69 1/2							13 1/2
DATE			U.S. STEEL						BETHLEHEM STEEL						KEY PRICE			
JAN. 23			57 7/8						63 3/4						121 5/8			
24			56 1/2						63 1/4						119 3/4			
25			55 5/8						63						118 5/8			
26			53 1/4						60 1/4						113 1/2			
27																		
SAT. 28																		
30																		
31		59 1/2						68 1/2						128				
FEB. 1																		
2		60												128 1/2				
3																		
SAT. 4		60 5/8						69						129 5/8				
6								69 7/8						130 1/4				
7																		
8																		
9																		
10																		
SAT. 11																		
14																		
15																		
16								70 3/4						131 5/8				
17		61 1/8						71 1/4						132 3/8				
SAT. 18		61 1/4												132 1/2				
20																		
21																		
23																		
24		62 1/4						72 3/8						139 5/8				
SAT. 25		63 3/4						74 3/4						138 1/2				
27																		
28		64 3/4						75						139 3/4				
MAR. 1																		
2																		
3		64 7/8						75 1/4						140				
SAT. 4								75 1/2						140 3/8				
6																		
7																		

On March 16th, prices of U. S. Steel and Bethlehem Steel were recorded in the Natural Reaction column. Refer to Explanatory Rule 6-B.

On March 30th, the price of U. S. Steel was recorded in the Downward Trend column, being a lower price than was previously recorded in the Downward Trend column.

On March 31st, the price of Bethlehem Steel was recorded in the Downward Trend column, being a lower price than was previously recorded in the Downward Trend column.

On April 15th, prices of U. S. Steel and Bethlehem Steel were recorded in the Natural Rally column. Refer to Explanatory Rule 6-C.

DATE	SECONDARY RALLY	NATURAL RALLY	UPWARD TREND	DOWNWARD TREND	NATURAL REACTION	SECONDARY REACTION	SECONDARY RALLY	NATURAL RALLY	UPWARD TREND	DOWNWARD TREND	NATURAL REACTION	SECONDARY REACTION	SECONDARY RALLY	NATURAL RALLY	UPWARD TREND	DOWNWARD TREND	NATURAL REACTION	SECONDARY REACTION
				$53\frac{1}{4}$				$60\frac{1}{4}$								$113\frac{1}{2}$		
1939		$64\frac{7}{8}$						$75\frac{1}{2}$						$140\frac{3}{8}$				
DATE		U.S. STEEL					BETHLEHEM STEEL						KEY PRICE					
MAR. 8		65												$140\frac{1}{2}$				
9		$65\frac{1}{2}$						$75\frac{7}{8}$						$141\frac{3}{8}$				
10																		
SAT. 11																		
13																		
14																		
15																		
16				$59\frac{5}{8}$						$69\frac{1}{4}$						$128\frac{7}{8}$		
17				$56\frac{3}{4}$						$66\frac{3}{4}$						$123\frac{1}{2}$		
SAT. 18				$54\frac{3}{4}$						65						$119\frac{3}{4}$		
20																		
21																		
22				$53\frac{1}{2}$						$63\frac{5}{8}$						$117\frac{1}{8}$		
23																		
24																		
SAT. 25																		
27																		
28																		
29																		
30				$52\frac{1}{8}$							62					$114\frac{1}{8}$		
31				$49\frac{7}{8}$						$58\frac{3}{4}$						$108\frac{5}{8}$		
APR. SAT. 1																		
3																		
4				$48\frac{1}{4}$						$57\frac{5}{8}$						$105\frac{7}{8}$		
5																		
6				$47\frac{1}{4}$						$55\frac{1}{2}$						$102\frac{3}{4}$		
SAT. 8				$44\frac{7}{8}$						$52\frac{1}{2}$						$97\frac{3}{8}$		
10																		
11				$44\frac{3}{8}$						$51\frac{5}{8}$						96		
12																		
13																		
14																		
SAT. 15		50						$58\frac{1}{2}$						$108\frac{1}{2}$				
17																		
18																		
19																		

97

On May 17th, prices of U. S. Steel and Bethlehem Steel were recorded in the Natural Reaction column, and the next day, May 18th, the price of U. S. Steel was recorded in the Downward Trend column. Refer to Explanatory Rule 6-D. The next day, May 19th, a red line was drawn under the Downward Trend column in Bethlehem Steel, meaning a price was made that was the same as the last price recorded in the Downward Trend column.

On May 25th, prices of U. S. Steel and Bethlehem Steel were recorded in the Secondary Rally column. Refer to Explanatory Rule 6-C.

Secondary Rally	Natural Rally	Upward Trend	Downward Trend	Natural Reaction	Secondary Reaction	Secondary Rally	Natural Rally	Upward Trend	Downward Trend	Natural Reaction	Secondary Reaction	Secondary Rally	Natural Rally	Upward Trend	Downward Trend	Natural Reaction	Secondary Reaction
		$44\frac{3}{8}$						$51\frac{5}{8}$							96		
1939	50						$58\frac{1}{2}$						$108\frac{1}{2}$				
DATE		U.S. STEEL				BETHLEHEM STEEL						KEY PRICE					
APR.20																	
21																	
SAT.22																	
24																	
25																	
26																	
27																	
28																	
SAT.29																	
MAY 1																	
2																	
3																	
4																	
5																	
SAT.6																	
8																	
9																	
10																	
11																	
12																	
SAT.13																	
15																	
16																	
17				$44\frac{5}{8}$							52						$96\frac{5}{8}$	
18			$43\frac{1}{4}$													$95\frac{1}{4}$		
19																$94\frac{7}{8}$		
SAT.20																	
22																	
23																	
24																	
25	$48\frac{3}{4}$						$57\frac{3}{4}$						$106\frac{1}{2}$					
26	49						58						107					
SAT.27	$49\frac{3}{8}$						—						$107\frac{7}{8}$					
29		$50\frac{1}{4}$						$59\frac{3}{8}$						$109\frac{5}{8}$				
31		$50\frac{7}{8}$						60						$110\frac{7}{8}$				
JUNE 1																		

99

On June 16th, the price of Bethlehem Steel was recorded in the Natural Reaction column. Refer to Explanatory Rule 6-B.

On June 28th, the price of U. S. Steel was recorded in the Natural Reaction column. Refer to Explanatory Rule 6-B.

On June 29th, the price of Bethlehem Steel was recorded in the Downward Trend column, being a price lower than the last price recorded in the Downward Trend column.

On July 13th, prices of U. S. Steel and Bethlehem Steel were recorded in the Secondary Rally column. Refer to Explanatory Rule 6-G.

DATE	SECONDARY RALLY	NATURAL RALLY	UPWARD TREND	DOWNWARD TREND	NATURAL REACTION	SECONDARY REACTION	SECONDARY RALLY	NATURAL RALLY	UPWARD TREND	DOWNWARD TREND	NATURAL REACTION	SECONDARY REACTION	SECONDARY RALLY	NATURAL RALLY	UPWARD TREND	DOWNWARD TREND	NATURAL REACTION	SECONDARY REACTION
				44 3/8						51 5/8						96		
		50						58 1/2						108 1/2				
				43 1/4						—							94 7/8	
1939		50 7/8						60						110 7/8				
DATE			U.S. STEEL					BETHLEHEM STEEL						KEY PRICE				
JUNE 2																		
SAT. 3																		
5																		
6																		
7																		
8																		
9																		
SAT. 10																		
12																		
13																		
14																		
15																		
16											54							
SAT. 17																		
19																		
20																		
21																		
22																		
23																		
SAT. 24																		
26																		
27																		
28					45						52 1/2							97 1/2	
29				43 3/4						51						94 3/4		
30				43 5/8						50 1/4						93 7/8		
SAT JULY 1																		
3																		
5																		
6																		
7																		
SAT. 8																		
10																		
11																		
12																		
13	48 1/4						57 1/4						105 1/2					
14																		

On July 21st, the price of Bethlehem Steel was recorded in the Upward Trend column, and the next day, July 22nd, the price of U. S. Steel was recorded in the Upward Trend column. Refer to Explanatory Rule 5-A.

On August 4th, prices of U. S. Steel and Bethlehem Steel were recorded in the Natural Reaction column. Refer to Explanatory Rule 4-A.

On August 23rd, the price of U. S. Steel was recorded in the Downward Trend column, being lower than the price previously recorded in the Downward Trend column.

DATE	SECONDARY RALLY	NATURAL RALLY	UPWARD TREND	DOWNWARD TREND	NATURAL REACTION	SECONDARY REACTION	SECONDARY RALLY	NATURAL RALLY	UPWARD TREND	DOWNWARD TREND	NATURAL REACTION	SECONDARY REACTION	SECONDARY RALLY	NATURAL RALLY	UPWARD TREND	DOWNWARD TREND	NATURAL REACTION	SECONDARY REACTION
				$43\frac{1}{4}$						$51\frac{5}{8}$						$94\frac{7}{8}$		
		$50\frac{7}{8}$						60						$110\frac{7}{8}$				
					$43\frac{5}{8}$						$50\frac{1}{4}$						$93\frac{7}{8}$	
1939	$48\frac{1}{4}$					$57\frac{1}{4}$							$105\frac{1}{2}$					
DATE		U.S. STEEL						BETHLEHEM STEEL						KEY PRICE				
SAT. JULY 15																		
17	$50\frac{3}{4}$						$60\frac{5}{8}$						$111\frac{1}{8}$					
18		$51\frac{7}{8}$						62						$113\frac{7}{8}$				
19																		
20																		
21	$52\frac{1}{2}$							63						$115\frac{1}{2}$				
SAT. 22		$54\frac{1}{8}$						65							$119\frac{1}{8}$			
24																		
25		$55\frac{1}{8}$						$65\frac{3}{4}$							$120\frac{7}{8}$			
26																		
27																		
28																		
SAT. 29																		
31																		
AUG. 1																		
2																		
3																		
4					$49\frac{1}{2}$						$59\frac{1}{2}$						109	
SAT. 5																		
7					$49\frac{1}{4}$												$108\frac{3}{4}$	
8																		
9											59						$108\frac{1}{4}$	
10					$47\frac{3}{4}$						58						$105\frac{3}{4}$	
11					47												105	
SAT. 12																		
14																		
15																		
16																		
17					$46\frac{1}{2}$												$104\frac{1}{2}$	
18					45						$55\frac{1}{8}$						$100\frac{1}{8}$	
SAT. 19																		
21					$43\frac{3}{8}$						$53\frac{3}{8}$						$96\frac{3}{4}$	
22																		
23				$42\frac{5}{8}$													96	
24				$41\frac{5}{8}$							$51\frac{7}{8}$					$93\frac{1}{2}$		
25																		

On August 29th, prices of U. S. Steel and Bethlehem Steel were recorded in the Natural Rally column. Refer to Explanatory Rule 6-D.

On September 2nd, prices of U. S. Steel and Bethlehem Steel were recorded in the Upward Trend column, being higher prices than the last prices previously recorded in the Upward Trend column.

On September 14th, prices of U. S. Steel and Bethlehem Steel were recorded in the Natural Reaction column. Refer to Explanatory Rules 6-A and 4-A.

On September 19th, prices of U. S. Steel and Bethlehem Steel were recorded in the Natural Rally column. Refer to Explanatory Rules 6-D and 4-B.

On September 28th, prices for U. S. Steel and Bethlehem Steel were recorded in the Secondary Reaction column. Refer to Explanatory Rule 6-H.

On October 6th, prices of U. S. Steel and Bethlehem Steel were recorded in the Secondary Rally column. Refer to Explanatory Rule 6-G.

CHART THIRTEEN

Date	SECONDARY RALLY	NATURAL RALLY	UPWARD TREND	DOWNWARD TREND	NATURAL REACTION	SECONDARY REACTION	SECONDARY RALLY	NATURAL RALLY	UPWARD TREND	DOWNWARD TREND	NATURAL REACTION	SECONDARY REACTION	SECONDARY RALLY	NATURAL RALLY	UPWARD TREND	DOWNWARD TREND	NATURAL REACTION	SECONDARY REACTION
				$43\frac{1}{4}$						$50\frac{1}{4}$						$93\frac{7}{8}$		
			$55\frac{1}{8}$						$65\frac{3}{4}$						$120\frac{7}{8}$			
1939			$41\frac{5}{8}$								$51\frac{7}{8}$				$93\frac{1}{2}$			
DATE			U.S. STEEL						BETHLEHEM STEEL						KEY PRICE			
SAT. AUG.26																		
28																		
29		48						$60\frac{1}{2}$						$108\frac{1}{2}$				
30																		
31																		
SEPT.1		52						$65\frac{1}{2}$						$117\frac{1}{2}$				
SAT.2			$55\frac{1}{4}$						$70\frac{3}{8}$						$125\frac{5}{8}$			
5			$66\frac{7}{8}$						$85\frac{1}{2}$						$152\frac{3}{8}$			
6																		
7																		
8			$69\frac{3}{4}$						87						$156\frac{3}{4}$			
SAT.9			70						$88\frac{1}{4}$						$158\frac{3}{4}$			
11			$78\frac{5}{8}$						100						$178\frac{5}{8}$			
12			$82\frac{3}{4}$												$182\frac{3}{4}$			
13																		
14				$76\frac{3}{8}$						$91\frac{1}{4}$						$168\frac{1}{8}$		
15																		
SAT.16				$75\frac{1}{2}$						$88\frac{3}{8}$						$163\frac{7}{8}$		
18				$70\frac{1}{2}$						$83\frac{3}{4}$						$154\frac{1}{4}$		
19		78						$92\frac{3}{8}$						$170\frac{3}{8}$				
20		$80\frac{5}{8}$						$95\frac{5}{8}$						$176\frac{1}{4}$				
21																		
22																		
SAT.23																		
25																		
26																		
27																		
28					$75\frac{1}{8}$						89						$164\frac{1}{8}$	
29					$73\frac{1}{2}$						$86\frac{3}{4}$						$160\frac{1}{4}$	
SAT.30																		
OCT.2																		
3																		
4					73						$86\frac{1}{4}$						$159\frac{1}{4}$	
5																		
6	$78\frac{1}{2}$						$92\frac{3}{4}$						$171\frac{1}{4}$					
SAT.7																		

On November 3rd, the price of U. S. Steel was recorded in the Secondary Reaction column, being a price lower than the last previous price recorded in that column.

On November 9th, a dash was made in the Natural Reaction column of U. S. Steel, being the same price that was last recorded in the Natural Reaction column, and on the same day a new price was recorded in the Natural Reaction column of Bethlehem Steel, being a lower price than the last price previously recorded in that column.

CHART FOURTEEN

	SECONDARY RALLY	NATURAL RALLY	UPWARD TREND	DOWNWARD TREND	NATURAL REACTION	SECONDARY REACTION	SECONDARY RALLY	NATURAL RALLY	UPWARD TREND	DOWNWARD TREND	NATURAL REACTION	SECONDARY REACTION	SECONDARY RALLY	NATURAL RALLY	UPWARD TREND	DOWNWARD TREND	NATURAL REACTION	SECONDARY REACTION
			82 3/4						100						182 3/4			
					70 1/2						83 3/4						154 1/4	
		80 5/8						95 5/8						176 1/4				
						73						86 1/4						159 1/4
1939	78 1/2						92 3/4						171 1/4					
DATE			U.S. STEEL							BETHLEHEM STEEL					KEY PRICE			
OCT. 9																		
10																		
11																		
13																		
SAT. 14																		
16																		
17	78 7/8						93 7/8						172 3/4					
18	79 1/4												173 1/2					
19																		
20																		
SAT. 21																		
23																		
24																		
25																		
26																		
27																		
SAT. 28																		
30																		
31																		
NOV. 1																		
2																		
3						72 1/2												
SAT. 4																		
6																		
8						72 1/8						86 1/8						158 1/4
9					—						83 1/4						153 3/4	
10					68 3/4						81 3/4						150 1/2	
13																		
14																		
15																		
16																		
17																		
SAT. 18																		
20																		
21																		
22																		

On November 24th, the price of U. S. Steel was recorded in the Downward Trend column. Refer to Explanatory Rule 6-E, and the next day, November 25th, the price of Bethlehem Steel was recorded in the Downward Trend column. Refer to Explanatory Rule 6-E.

On December 7th, prices of U. S. Steel and Bethlehem Steel were recorded in the Natural Rally column. Refer to Explanatory Rule 6-C.

DATE	SECONDARY RALLY	NATURAL RALLY	UPWARD TREND	DOWNWARD TREND	NATURAL REACTION	SECONDARY REACTION	SECONDARY RALLY	NATURAL RALLY	UPWARD TREND	DOWNWARD TREND	NATURAL REACTION	SECONDARY REACTION	SECONDARY RALLY	NATURAL RALLY	UPWARD TREND	DOWNWARD TREND	NATURAL REACTION	SECONDARY REACTION
			$82\frac{3}{4}$						100						$182\frac{3}{4}$			
				$70\frac{1}{2}$							$83\frac{3}{4}$						$154\frac{1}{4}$	
		$80\frac{5}{8}$						$95\frac{5}{8}$						$176\frac{1}{4}$				
1939 DATE			$68\frac{3}{4}$							$81\frac{3}{4}$						$150\frac{1}{2}$	
		U.S. STEEL					BETHLEHEM STEEL						KEY PRICE				
NOV 24			$66\frac{7}{8}$								81			$147\frac{7}{8}$				
SAT. 25										$80\frac{3}{4}$				$147\frac{5}{8}$				
27																		
28																		
29			$65\frac{7}{8}$								$78\frac{1}{8}$			144				
30			$63\frac{5}{8}$								77			$140\frac{5}{8}$				
DEC. 1																		
SAT. 2																		
4																		
5																		
6																		
7	$69\frac{3}{4}$							84						$53\frac{3}{4}$				
8																		
SAT. 9																		
11																		
12																		
13																		
14									$84\frac{7}{8}$						$54\frac{5}{8}$				
15																		
SAT. 16																		
18																		
19																		
20																		
21																		
22																		
SAT. 23																		
26																		
27																		
28																		
29																		
SAT. 30																		
1940 JAN. 2																		
3																		
4																		
5																		
SAT. 6																		

On January 9th, prices of U.S. Steel and Bethlehem Steel were recorded in the Natural Reaction column. Refer to Explanatory Rule 6-B.

On January 11th, prices of U. S. Steel and Bethlehem Steel were recorded in the Downward Trend column, being prices lower than the last recorded prices in the Downward Trend columns.

On February 7th, prices are recorded in the Natural Rally column of Bethlehem Steel, this being the first day it rallied the required distance of six points. The following day U. S. Steel is recorded in addition to Bethlehem Steel and the Key Price, the latter having rallied the proper distance to be used in recording.

Date	SECONDARY RALLY	NATURAL RALLY	UPWARD TREND	DOWNWARD TREND	NATURAL REACTION	SECONDARY REACTION	SECONDARY RALLY	NATURAL RALLY	UPWARD TREND	DOWNWARD TREND	NATURAL REACTION	SECONDARY REACTION	SECONDARY RALLY	NATURAL RALLY	UPWARD TREND	DOWNWARD TREND	NATURAL REACTION	SECONDARY REACTION
				$63\frac{5}{8}$						77						$140\frac{5}{8}$		
1940		$69\frac{3}{4}$						$84\frac{7}{8}$						$154\frac{5}{8}$				
			U.S. STEEL						BETHLEHEM STEEL						KEY PRICE			
JAN.8																		
9				$64\frac{1}{4}$							$78\frac{1}{2}$						$142\frac{3}{4}$	
10				$63\frac{3}{4}$													$142\frac{1}{4}$	
11				62						$76\frac{1}{2}$						$138\frac{1}{2}$		
12				$60\frac{1}{8}$						$74\frac{1}{8}$						$134\frac{1}{4}$		
SAT.13				$59\frac{5}{8}$						$73\frac{1}{2}$						$133\frac{1}{8}$		
15				$57\frac{1}{2}$						72						$129\frac{1}{2}$		
16																		
17																		
18				$56\frac{7}{8}$						$71\frac{1}{2}$						$128\frac{3}{8}$		
19										71						$127\frac{7}{8}$		
SAT.20																		
22				$55\frac{7}{8}$						$70\frac{1}{8}$						126		
23																		
24																		
25																		
26																		
SAT.27																		
29																		
30																		
31																		
FEB.1																		
2																		
SAT.3																		
5																		
6																		
7									$76\frac{3}{8}$									
8		61						78						139				
9		$61\frac{3}{4}$						$79\frac{1}{2}$						$141\frac{1}{4}$				
SAT.10																		
13																		
14																		
15																		
16				$56\frac{1}{8}$														
SAT.17																		
19																		

MARKET ART!

The painting pictured on the back cover of this book, as well as other Market-related art, is available through **TRADERS PRESS.**

If interested in full details, please contact:

TRADERS PRESS™
P.O. Box 6206
Greenville, S.C. 29606

Books and Gifts
for Investors and Traders